Playtime
ROMPERS to KNIT

Playtime
ROMPERS to KNIT

25 Cute Comfy Patterns for Babies plus 2 Matching Doll Rompers

JESSICA ANDERSON

STACKPOLE BOOKS

Guilford, Connecticut
Blue Ridge Summit, Pennsylvania

STACKPOLE BOOKS

An imprint of Globe Pequot, the trade division of The Rowman & Littlefield Publishing Group, Inc.
4501 Forbes Blvd., Ste. 200
Lanham, MD 20706
www.rowman.com

Distributed by NATIONAL BOOK NETWORK
800-462-6420

British Library Cataloguing in Publication Information available

Library of Congress Cataloging-in-Publication Data Available

Names: Anderson, Jessica, 1982- author.
Title: Playtime rompers to knit : 25 cute comfy patterns for babies plus 2
    matching doll rompers / Jessica Anderson.
Description: First edition. | Guilford, Connecticut : Stackpole Books,
    [2022] | Includes index.
Identifiers: LCCN 2021056566 (print) | LCCN 2021056567 (ebook) | ISBN
    9780811739481 (paperback) | ISBN 9780811769426 (epub)
Subjects: LCSH: Knitting--Patterns. | Rompers (Clothing) | Infants'
    clothing. | Animals in art.
Classification: LCC TT825 .A5355 2022 (print) | LCC TT825 (ebook) | DDC
    746.43/2041--dc23/eng/20211209
LC record available at https://lccn.loc.gov/2021056566
LC ebook record available at https://lccn.loc.gov/2021056567

♾™ The paper used in this publication meets the minimum requirements of American National Standard for Information Sciences—Permanence of Paper for Printed Library Materials, ANSI/NISO Z39.48-1992.

First Edition

CONTENTS

PREFACE

As I write today, I'm currently snuggled in bed next to my smallest little one, who is teething and miserable with a runny nose and low-grade fever, and overall just in need of Mommy. Some days, this happens. Everything else just gets put on hold, the laundry piles up, and the "me-time" becomes snuggle-in-bed time. Of course, there are knitting magazines, a tablet, and some yarn nearby, as well as my water, some snacks, and the remote (I'm no novice; I'm in for the long haul!), but for now, my focus is on my little guy and helping him feel better. While he snoozes, my mind wanders, and I know that there is nothing more important that I need to do today than just to be there for him—whether by simply snuggling in bed with him or holding him while he sleeps and nursing him when he wakes up hungry and tearful. I'm there for him, and, when I need it, my knitting is there for me.

The yarn and needles just sit there, content to wait their turn, to offer a silent nod of comfort and solace. They are never demanding or impatient, they just wait for me and when I'm ready, they are ready, like a familiar and comforting sweater just begging to be worn when you need it, giving you warmth, comfort, and security. That's knitting for you.

When you have little ones, the days can be long, but the years are so incredibly short. Sometimes you might feel like it's a waste to spend a day in bed, reading that silly rhyme book for the umpteenth time, or you might have just had your fill of dog-themed movies by lunchtime, but rest assured, one day (not anytime soon, I promise!), this will be a fleeting memory. And when that day comes, the yarn and needles will be there as well. Don't buy in to the hype either: you don't have to be Supermom—some days you're just Mom, and that's OK. If you aren't resting, eating, and taking care of yourself, you can't nurse, comfort, and take care of others, no matter what the commercials try to tell you.

Practicing self-care can be very difficult, especially when there's so much to do and so little time to get it all done. Knitting is always there—never demanding, never begging, and always offering comfort, rest, and quiet. As the days go rushing by, why not take a little time to make memories, to piece together fabrics that will not only bring you joy and pride in their creation, but will bring laughter, smiles, and memories from your kids? And when all is said and done, the time and beauty will wrap you in your own blanket to hold you when you're sick, to bring you comfort when you're lonely, and to be there when you just need a minute to remember that you are loved and cherished. The knitting—it will always be there, it will always wait for you, and it will always offer you a gift you didn't know you wanted but appreciate so very much.

1 The Basics

BASIC Romper

When you just want to grab something and get started, this Basic Romper is where it's at! This is like the cookie recipe you turn to over and over again—your knitting pantry staple. All the other rompers are basically a variation in one form or another of this one.

Sizes: Newborn (6 months, 12 months, 18 months)

Finished Chest Circumference: 16 (18, 19, 20) in / 40.5 (45.5, 48.5, 51) cm

Gauge: 24 sts and 32 rows = 4 in / 10 cm in St st on larger needles, after washing and blocking

Yarn: Tippy Tree Yarns, Tippy Sport (#2 fine weight; 80% superwash merino, 20% nylon; 328 yd / 300 m per 3.5 oz / 100 g): 1 (1, 2, 2) skeins Unicorn Eyelashes

Needles: US 5 (3.75 mm) 16 in / 40 cm circular and dpn(s), or size needed to obtain gauge; and US 3 (3.25 mm) 16 in / 40 cm circular and dpn(s), or needles two sizes smaller than size needed to obtain gauge

Notions: Tapestry needle, two ½ in / 1.5 cm JHB buttons, sewing needle and thread, waste yarn

Stitch Guide

K1, P1 RIB WORKED FLAT

Row 1: *K1, p1; rep from * to end of row.
Row 2: *P1, k1; rep from * to end of row.
Repeat Rows 1 and 2 for Pattern.

K1, P1 RIB IN THE ROUND

Rnd 1: *K1, p1; rep from * to end of rnd.
Repeat Rnd 1 for Pattern.

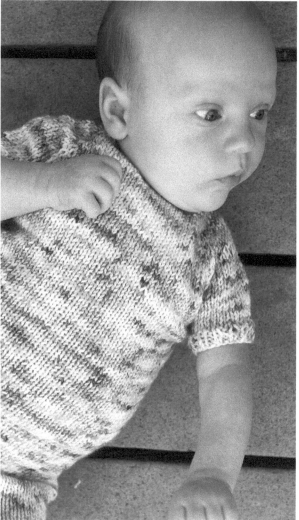

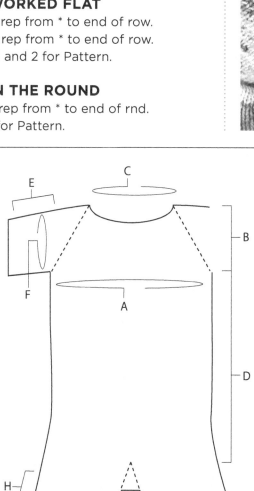

A - 16 (18, 19, 20) in
    40.5 (45.5, 48.5, 51) cm
B - 3.75 (4.25, 4.25, 4.5) in
    9.5 (11, 11, 11.5) cm
C - 7.75 (8.5, 9.5, 10.5) in
    19.5 (21.5, 24, 26.5) cm
D - 10.5 (13.5, 14.5, 15.5) in
    26.5 (34.5, 37, 39.5) cm
E - 1.5 (1.5, 1.25, 1.5) in
    4 (4, 3, 4) cm
F - 6 (6.75, 7, 7.25) in
    15 (17, 18, 18.5) cm
G - 9.25 (10.25, 10.75, 11.25) in
    23.5 (26, 27.5, 28.5) cm
H - 3 (3.5, 3.75, 4) in
    7.5 (9, 9.5, 10) cm

INSTRUCTIONS

Body

With smaller needles, CO 47 (51, 57, 63) sts.

Set-up Row 1 (RS): K11 (11, 13, 13) front sts, pm, k6 (6, 6, 8) sleeve sts, pm, k16 (20, 22, 24) back sts, pm, k6 (6, 6, 8) sleeve sts, pm, k8 (8, 10, 10) front sts.

Set-up Row 2 (WS): Knit.

Set-up Row 3: Knit.

Buttonhole Row (WS): Knit to last 3 sts, k2tog, yo, k1.

Switch to larger needles.

Inc Row (RS): (Knit to 1 st before m, k1f&b, sm, k1f&b) 4 times, knit to end—55 (59, 65, 71) sts.

Even Row (WS): K3, purl to last 3 sts, k3 (slipping all markers as you come to them).

Next Inc Row (RS): (Knit to 1 st before m, k1f&b, sm, k1f&b) 4 times, knit to end—63 (67, 73, 79) sts.

Buttonhole Row (WS): K3, purl to last 3 sts, k2tog, yo, k1.

Next Inc Row (RS): (Knit to 1 st before m, k1f&b, sm, k1f&b) 4 times, knit to end—71 (75, 81, 87) sts.

Next Row: K3, purl to last 3 sts, k3.

Joining Rnd (RS): Slip 3 sts purlwise from the RH needle to spare dpn, then k2tog using 1 st from RH needle and 1 st from dpn three times. Join to work in the round and place a different type of marker to distinguish the start of the round, (knit to 1 st before m, k1f&b, sm, k1f&b) 4 times, knit to end of rnd—76 (80, 86, 92) sts.

Even Rnd: Knit.

Inc Rnd: (Knit to 1 st before m, k1f&b, sm, k1f&b) 4 times, knit to end—84 (88, 94, 100) sts.

Repeat last 2 rnds 10 (12, 12, 13) times—164 (184, 190, 204) sts.

Separate Sleeves: Knit to 1st m, remove m, slip 36 (40, 40, 44) sleeve sts to waste yarn, CO 2 sts, remove m, knit to next marker, remove m, slip 36 (40, 40, 44) sleeve sts to waste yarn, CO 2 sts, remove m, knit to end of rnd—96 (108, 114, 120) sts.

Knit even until piece measures 10.5 (13.5, 14.5, 15.5) in / 26.5 (34.5, 37, 39.5) cm from underarm.

Gusset

Set-up Rnd: K1, place gusset marker, k46 (52, 55, 58), place gusset marker, k2, place gusset marker, knit to 1 st before BOR, place gusset marker, k1.

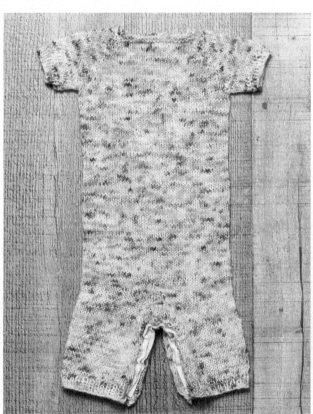
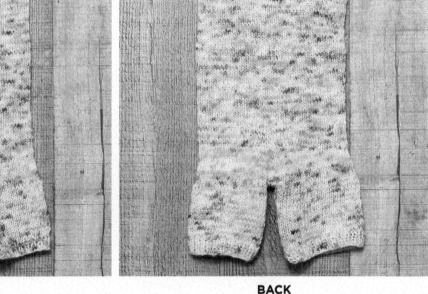

FRONT   **BACK**

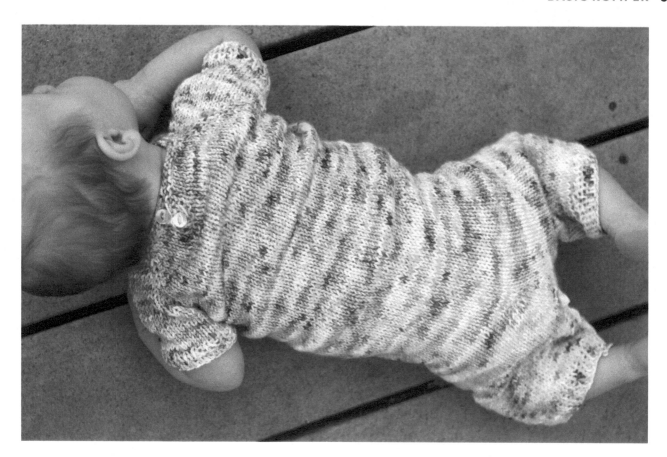

Inc Rnd: Knit to gusset m, m1L, sm, knit to next gusset m, sm, m1R, knit to next gusset m, M1L, sm, knit to next gusset m, sm, M1R, knit to end.

Repeat last 2 rnds until there are 11 sts between each set of gusset markers.

Split Legs: Knit to last gusset marker, slip next 11 sts to waste yarn, turn and purl back to the back gusset sts, slip next 11 sts to waste yarn. Continue working left leg only in St st flat, until leg measures 2 (2.5, 2.75, 3) in / 5 (6.5, 7, 7.5) cm from split.

Note: If preferred here, you can place the right leg sts on waste yarn or a holder, but you can easily leave them on the other portion of the circular needle while working the left leg flat.

Change to smaller needles, and work K1, P1 Rib for 1 in / 2.5 cm. Bind off in Rib pattern.

Repeat for second leg.

Gusset Snap Band: With smaller needles and the RS of the romper front facing, start at the bottom right corner, and pick up and knit 2 sts for every 3 rows along the leg, move the 11 held sts onto spare needles and knit across, pick up and knit 2 sts for every 3 rows down left side. Knit every row for 1.5 in / 4 cm. Bind off in Rib pattern. Repeat for back side.

Sleeves

Move 36 (40, 40, 44) sleeve sts to dpn(s). Knit around sleeve sts, pick up and knit 2 sts, pm, pick up and knit 2 sts.

Knit 3 rnds.

Dec Rnd: K1, k2tog, knit to last 3 sts before m, ssk, k1—2 sts dec.

Even Rnd: Knit.

Rep Dec Rnd 1 (1, 0, 1) time more—36 (40, 42, 44) sts.

Switch to smaller needles and work in K1, P1 Rib in the round for 3 rnds.

Bind off in Rib pattern.

FINISHING

Sew buttons carefully on button band on opposite side matching buttonholes.

Using a sewing machine or needle and thread, carefully sew snap tape along the RS of the gusset snap band.

Weave in all ends. Wash and block to measurements.

BASIC *Stripes*

When you want something just a little bit snazzier than your basic romper, and you have the time to make the magic—it's time for stripes! You can work any combination of stripes (this would be a super-fun time to make a magical-colored romper with all your leftover bits of yarn!), or you could use a super-dainty palette in shades of pink. I've paired a turquoise with a bright red in this piece for optimum fun and 110% style.

Sizes: Newborn (6 months, 12 months, 18 months)

Finished Chest Circumference: 16 (18, 20, 22) in / 40.5 (45.5, 51, 56) cm

Gauge: 20 sts and 28 rows = 4 in / 10 cm in St st on larger needles

Yarn: Lion Brand Yarn, Basic Stitch Premium (#4 medium weight; 100% acrylic; 219 yd / 200 m per 3.5 oz / 100 g): 1 (1, 2, 2) skeins Garnet (C1), and 1 (1, 2, 2) skeins Tourmaline (C2)

Needles: US 7 (4.5 mm) 16 in / 40 cm circular, or size needed to obtain gauge; and US 5 (3.75 mm) 16 in / 40 cm circular and dpn(s), or needles two sizes smaller than size needed to obtain gauge

Notions: Tapestry needle, three ½ in / 1.5 cm JBH buttons, 1 in / 2.5 cm wide snap tape, sewing thread, waste yarn

Stitch Guide

K1, P1 RIB WORKED FLAT
Row 1: *K1, p1; rep from * to end of row.
Row 2: *P1, k1; rep from * to end of row.
Repeat Rows 1 and 2 for pattern.

K1, P1 RIB IN THE ROUND
Rnd 1: *K1, p1; rep from * to end of rnd.
Repeat Rnd 1 for pattern.

STRIPE PATTERN
2 rows/rnds in C1
2 rows/rnds in C2
Stripe pattern is worked throughout pattern unless specified to work a particular color.

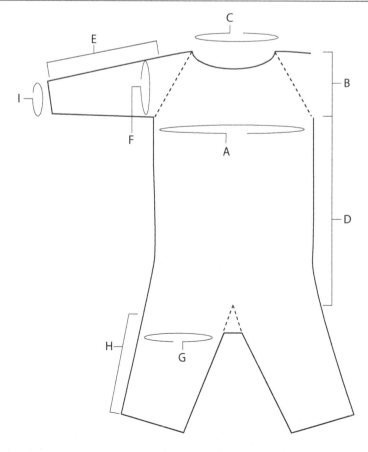

A - 16 (18, 20, 22) in
40.5 (45.5, 51, 56) cm
B - 2.75 (3.5, 4, 4.5) in
7 (9, 10, 11.5) cm
C - 9.75 (10.25, 11, 11.75) in
25 (26, 28, 30) cm
D - 10.5 (13.5, 14.5, 15.5) in
26.5 (34.5, 37, 39.5) cm
E - 7.5 (8.25, 9, 10) in
19 (21, 23, 25.5) cm
F - 6 (6.75, 7.75, 8.75) in
15 (17, 19.5, 22) cm
G - 8.25 (9, 9.75, 10.75) in
21 (23, 25, 27.5) cm
H - 5.5 (6.5, 7.5, 8.5) in
14 (16.5, 19, 21.5) cm
I - 4.75 (5.5, 6.5, 7.5) in
12 (14, 16.5, 19) cm

INSTRUCTIONS

Body

With larger needles and C1, CO 49 (51, 55, 59) sts.

Set-up Row 1 (RS): K5 sts (button band), pm, k6 (6, 7, 7) front sts, pm, k6 (6, 7, 8) sleeve sts, pm, k15 (17, 17, 19) back sts, pm, k6 (6, 7, 8) sleeve sts, pm, k6 (6, 7, 7) front sts, pm, k5 sts (button band).

Set-up Row 2 (WS): K5, purl to last 5 sts, k5 (slipping all markers as you come to them).

On next row switch to C2. Continue the striping pattern as listed above (switching every two rows) unless otherwise directed.

Inc Row (RS): K5, sm, (knit to 1 st before m, k1f&b sm, k1f&b) 4 times, knit to end of row— 57 (59, 63, 67) sts.

Even Row (WS): K5, purl to last 5 sts, k5 (slipping all markers as you come to them).

Buttonhole Inc Row (RS): K2, yo, k2tog, k1, sm, (knit to 1st before m, k1f&b, sm, k1f&b) 4 times, knit to end of row—65 (67, 71, 75) sts.

Even Row (WS): K5, purl to last 5 sts, k5 (slipping all markers as you come to them).

Inc Row (RS): K5, sm, (knit to 1 st before m, k1f&b sm, k1f&b) 4 times, knit to end of row—8 sts increased.

Repeat last two rows 2 (3, 4, 5) times more—89 (99, 111, 123) sts.

Work one more WS Even Row.

Buttonhole Inc Row (RS): K2, yo, k2tog, k1, sm, (knit to 1st before m, k1f&b, sm, k1f&b) 4 times, knit to end of row—97 (107, 119, 131) sts.

Even Row (WS): K5, purl to last 5 sts, k5 (slipping all markers as you come to them).

Inc Row (RS): K5, sm, (knit to 1 st before m, k1f&b sm, k1f&b) 4 times, knit to end of row—8 sts increased.

Repeat last two rows 1 (2, 3, 4) times more—113 (131, 151, 171) sts.

Work one more WS Even Row.

Buttonhole Inc Row (RS): K2, yo, k2tog, k1, sm, (knit to 1st before m, k1f&b, sm, k1f&b) 4 times, knit to end of row—121 (139, 159, 179) sts.

Even Row (WS): K5, purl to last 5 sts, k5 (slipping all markers as you come to them).

Join Fronts and Back (RS): K5, sm, (knit to 1 st before m, k1f&b sm, k1f&b) 4 times, knit to last 5 sts. Slip 5 sts purlwise from the LH needle

FRONT

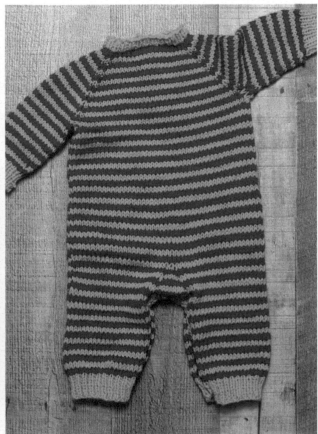

BACK

to spare dpn, then k2tog using 1 st from RH needle and 1 st from dpn five times—124 (142, 162, 182) sts.

Cut yarn, leaving a 12 in / 30.5 cm tail, slip 16 (18, 21, 23) sts purlwise to the RH needle (all the sts before the first sleeve m).

Separate Sleeves: Remove m, then move 26 (30, 35, 40) sleeve sts to waste yarn, CO 2 sts, place new BOR m, CO 2 sts, remove m, knit to next m, remove m, move 26 (30, 35, 40) sleeve sts to waste yarn, CO 2 sts, pm, CO 2 sts, knit to end of rnd.

Knit every rnd until piece measures 10.5 (13.5, 14.5, 15.5) in / 26.5 (34.5, 37, 39.5) cm from underarm.

Gusset

Set-up Rnd 1: K19 (22, 24, 27) sts, place gusset m, k1, place gusset m, k39 (44, 49, 54) sts, place gusset m, k1, place gusset m, knit to end.

Set-up Rnd 2: Knit.

Gusset Inc Rnd: Knit to gusset m, sm, *m1L, knit to m, m1R, sm; rep from * once, knit to end.

Even Rnd: Knit.

Repeat last 2 rnds four times more, until there are 11 sts between the gusset markers.

Split Legs: Knit to last gusset m, slip next 11 sts to waste yarn, turn and purl back to the back gusset sts, slip next 11 sts to waste yarn. Continue working left leg only in St st flat, until leg measures 4 (5, 6, 7) in / 10 (12.5, 15, 18) cm from split.

Note: If preferred here, you can place the right leg sts on waste yarn or a holder, but you can easily leave them on the other portion of the circular needle while working the left leg flat.

Switch to smaller needles and work in k1, p1 rib for 1.5 in / 4 cm.

Gusset Snap Band: With smaller needles and RS facing and starting at the bottom right corner of the front above the Rib stitch, pick up and knit 2 sts for every 3 sts along the leg, move the 11 held gusset sts on to spare needles and knit across, pick up and knit 2 sts for every 3 sts along the leg. Knit every row for 1.5 in / 4 cm. Bind off all sts. Repeat for back side.

Sleeves

Move 26 (30, 35, 40) sleeve sts to dpns.

Reattach yarn and knit around sleeve sts, pick up and knit 2 sts, pm, pick up and knit 2 sts—30 (34, 39, 44) sts.

Knit 3 rnds.

Dec Rnd: K1, k2tog, knit to last 3 sts before m, ssk, k1—28 (32, 37, 42) sts.

Knit 10 (10, 12, 14) rnds.

Dec Rnd: K1, k2tog, knit to last 3 sts before m, ssk, k1—26 (30, 35, 40) sts.

Knit 10 (10, 12, 14) rnds.

Dec Rnd: K1, k2tog, knit to last 3 sts before m, ssk, k1—24 (28, 33, 38) sts.

Knit until sleeve measures 5.5 (6.25, 7, 8, 9) in / 14 (16, 18, 20.5, 23) cm from underarm.

Final Dec Rnd (Size 12 Month Only): K1, k2tog, knit to end—24 (28, 32, 38) sts.

Switch to smaller needles and work in K1, P1 Rib for 2 in / 5 cm.

NECK EDGING

With smaller needles, starting at the back of the neck, pick up and knit 2 sts for every 3 sts around neck edge. Work in K1, P1 Rib for 3 rows. Bind off all sts in Rib pattern.

FINISHING

Sew buttons carefully on button band on opposite side matching buttonholes.

Using a sewing machine or needle and thread, carefully sew snap tape along the RS of the gusset snap band.

Weave in all ends. Wash and block to measurements.

BASIC *Hooded Romper*

This pattern takes your Basic Romper and ramps it up just a notch by adding a hood! Once you get the Basic Romper down, you can play around with making your hood really pop. This is a fun pattern with which to play around with yarn choices, or you can go with the recommended yarn and it does all the hard work of switching up colors and creating a stunning gradient for you.

Sizes: Newborn (6 months, 12 months, 18 months)

Finished Chest Circumference: 16 (18, 19, 20) in / 40.5 (45.5, 48.5, 51) cm

Gauge: 20 sts and 28 rows = 4 in / 10 cm in St st on larger needles

Yarn: Lion Brand Yarn, Ice Cream (#3 light weight; 100% acrylic; 394 yd / 360 m per 3.5 oz / 100 g): 2 (2, 2, 3) skeins Lemon Swirl

Needles: US 5 (3.75 mm) 16 in / 40 cm circular, or size needed to obtain gauge; US 4 (3.5 mm) 16 in / 40 cm circular and dpn(s), or needles one size smaller than size needed to obtain gauge

Notions: Tapestry needle, three ½ in / 1.5 cm JBH buttons, 1 in / 2.5 cm wide snap tape, sewing machine or needle and sewing thread, waste yarn

Stitch Guide

K1, P1 RIB WORKED FLAT
Row 1: *K1, p1; rep from * to end of row.
Row 2: *P1, k1; rep from * to end of row.
Repeat Rows 1 and 2 for pattern.

K1, P1 RIB IN THE ROUND
Rnd 1: *K1, p1; rep from * to end of rnd.
Repeat Rnd 1 for pattern.

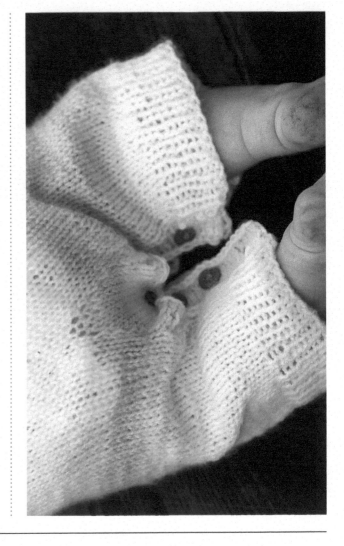

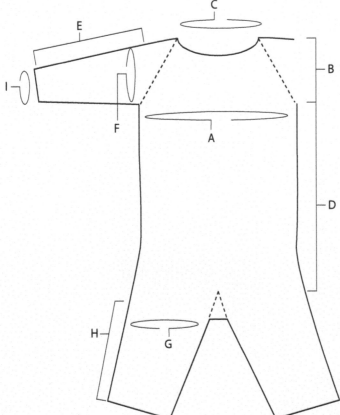

A - 16 (18, 19, 20) in
    40.5 (45.5, 48.5, 51) cm
B - 3.25 (3.75, 4, 4.25) in
    8.5 (9.5, 10, 11) cm
C - 9.5 (10.25, 10.75, 11.5) in
    24 (26, 27.5, 29) cm
D - 10.5 (13.5, 14.5, 15.5) in
    26.5 (34.5, 37, 39.5) cm
E - 7.5 (8.25, 9, 10) in
    19 (21, 23, 25.5) cm
F - 6.25 (7.25, 7.75, 8.5) in
    16 (18.5, 19.5, 21.5) cm
G - 8.25 (9, 9.5, 9.75) in
    21 (23, 24, 25) cm
H - 5.5 (6.5, 7.5, 8.5) in
    14 (16.5, 19, 21.5) cm
I - 5 (6, 6.5, 7.25) in
    12.5 (15, 16.5, 18.5) cm

INSTRUCTIONS

Body

With larger needles, CO 47 (51, 54, 57) sts.

Set-up Row 1 (RS): K5 sts (button band), pm, k6 front sts, pm, k5 (6, 7, 8) sleeve sts, pm, 15 (17, 18, 19) back sts, pm, k5 (6, 7, 8) sleeve sts, pm, k6 front sts, pm, k5 sts (button band).

Set-up Row 2 (WS): K5, purl to last 5 sts, k5 (slipping all markers as you come to them).

Inc Row (RS): K5, sm, (knit to 1 st before m, k1f&b sm, k1f&b) 4 times, knit to end of row—55 (59, 62, 65) sts.

Even Row (WS): K5, purl to last 5 sts, k5 (slipping all markers as you come to them).

Buttonhole Inc Row (RS): K2, yo, k2tog, k1, sm, (knit to 1st before m, k1f&b, sm, k1f&b) 4 times, knit to end of row—63 (67, 70, 73) sts.

Even Row (WS): K5, purl to last 5 sts, k5 (slipping all markers as you come to them).

Inc Row (RS): K5, sm, (knit to 1 st before m, k1f&b sm, k1f&b) 4 times, knit to end of row—8 sts increased.

Repeat last two rows 2 (3, 4, 4) times more—87 (99, 110, 113) sts.

Work one more WS Even Row.

Buttonhole Inc Row (RS): K2, yo, k2tog, k1, sm, (knit to 1st before m, k1f&b, sm, k1f&b) 4 times, knit to end of row—95 (107, 118, 121) sts.

Even Row (WS): K5, purl to last 5 sts, k5 (slipping all markers as you come to them).

Inc Row (RS): K5, sm, (knit to 1 st before m, k1f&b sm, k1f&b) 4 times, knit to end of row—8 sts increased.

Repeat last two rows 2 (3, 3, 4) times more—119 (139, 150, 161) sts.

Work one more WS Even Row.

Buttonhole Inc Row (RS): K2, yo, k2tog, k1, sm, (knit to 1st before m, k1f&b, sm, k1f&b) 4 times, knit to end of row—127 (147, 158, 169) sts.

Even Row (WS): K5, purl to last 5 sts, k5 (slipping all markers as you come to them).

Join Fronts and Back (RS): K5, sm, (knit to 1 st before m, k1f&b sm, k1f&b) 4 times, knit to last 5 sts. Slip 5 sts purlwise from the LH needle to spare dpn, then k2tog using 1 st from the RH needle and 1 st from dpn five times—130 (150, 161, 172) sts.

Separate Sleeves: Remove m, knit to next m, then move 27 (32, 35, 38) sleeve sts to waste yarn, CO 1 st, place new BOR m, CO 1 st, remove m, knit to next m, remove m, move 27

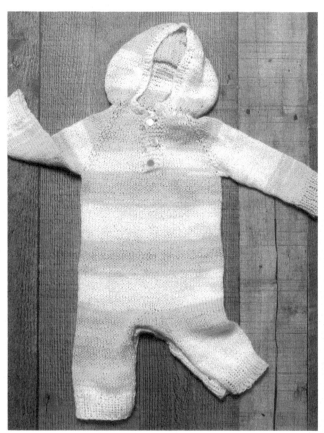

FRONT

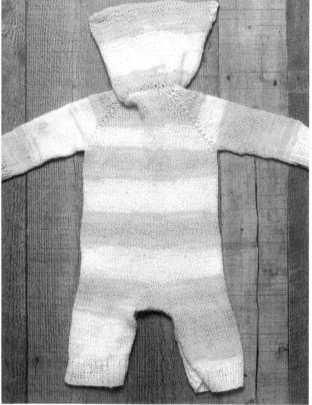

BACK

(32, 35, 38) sleeve sts to waste yarn, CO 1 st, pm, CO 1 st, knit to end of rnd.

Knit every rnd until piece measures 10.5 (13.5, 14.5, 15.5) in / 26.5 (34.5, 37, 39.5) cm from underarm.

Gusset

Set-up Rnd 1: K19 (22, 23, 25) sts, place gusset m, k1, place gusset m, k40 (45, 48, 50) sts, place gusset m, k1, place gusset m, knit to end.

Set-up Rnd 2: Knit.

Gusset Inc Rnd: Knit to gusset m, sm, *m1L, knit to m, m1R, sm; rep from * once, knit to end.

Even Rnd: Knit.

Repeat last 2 rnds four times more, until there are 11 sts between the gusset markers.

Split Legs: Knit to last gusset m, slip next 11 sts to waste yarn, turn and purl back to back gusset sts, slip next 11 sts to waste yarn. Continue working left leg only in St st flat, until leg measures 2 (2, 3, 3) in / 5 (5, 7.5, 7.5) cm from split.

Note: If preferred here, you can place the right leg sts on waste yarn or a holder, but you can easily leave them on the other portion of the circular needle while working the left leg flat.

Switch to smaller needles and work in k1, p1 rib for 1.5 in / 4 cm.

Gusset Snap Band: With smaller needles and RS facing and starting at the bottom right corner of the front above the Rib stitch, pick up and knit 2 sts for every 3 sts along the leg, move the 11 held gusset sts on to spare needles and knit across, pick up and knit 2 sts for every 3 sts along the leg. Knit every row for 1.5 in / 4 cm. Bind off all sts. Repeat for back side.

Sleeves

Move 27 (32, 35, 38) sleeve sts to dpns.

Reattach yarn and knit around sleeve sts, pick up and knit 2 sts, pm, pick up and knit 2 sts—31 (36, 39, 42) sts.

Knit 3 rnds.

Dec Rnd: K1, k2tog, knit to last 3 sts before m, ssk, k1—29 (34, 37, 40) sts.

Knit 10 (10, 12, 14) rnds.

Dec Rnd: K1, k2tog, knit to last 3 sts before m, ssk, k1—27 (32, 35, 38) sts.

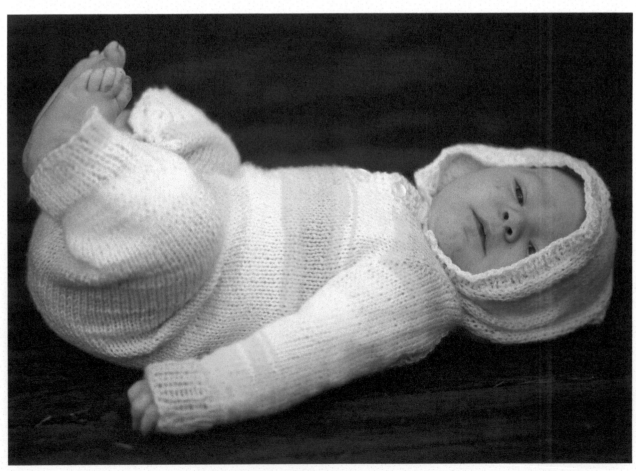

Knit 10 (10, 12, 14) rnds.

Dec Rnd: K1, k2tog, knit to last 3 sts before m, ssk, k1—25 (30, 33, 36) sts.

Knit until sleeve measures 5.5 (6.25, 7, 8) in / 14 (16, 17, 20.5) cm from underarm.

Final Dec Rnd (Sizes Newborn and 12 Months Only): K1, k2tog, knit to end—24 (30, 32, 36) sts.

Switch to smaller needles and work in K1, P1 Rib for 2 in / 5 cm.

Hood

Begin at right front edge with larger needles, pick up and knit 36 (40, 40, 44) sts.

Next Row (WS): Purl.

Inc Row 1 (RS): *K1, k1f&b; rep from * to end— 54 (60, 60, 66) sts.

Next Row: Purl.

Inc Row 2: *K2, k1f&b; rep from * to end of row—72 (80, 80, 88) sts.

Work in St st until hood measures 7 (7, 7.5, 8) in / 18 (18, 19, 20.5) cm.

Using Kitchener stitch, graft hood closed.

HOOD EDGING

With smaller needles and beginning at right front edge after the button band, pick up and knit around the fronts, the hood, and the left front.

Work in K1, P1 Rib for 3 rows. Bind off in Rib pattern.

FINISHING

Using a sewing machine or needle and thread, sew snap tape on the gusset snap band.

Sew buttons opposite buttonholes.

Weave in all ends. Wash and block.

A SPECIAL *Little Pocket*

I remember when my middle child was just a baby and he had the sweetest romper, made even more adorable by a strategically placed "bum" flap! In my sleep-deprived state, I wasn't quite sure what it was for, but as soon as that inevitable next diaper change came around, it hit me, it was a quick-change option. This cozy romper is worked in one piece to the "pocket" separation, if you will. Since you have an easy access for changes with the back pocket, the legs are worked in the round, and the gusset is seamed together (much like you would work on a pair of longies). This change is a fantastic option if you are up for something just a little bit different, and totally snazzy.

Sizes: Newborn (6 months, 12 months, 18 months)

Finished Chest Circumference: 16 (18, 20, 22) in / 40.5 (45.5, 51, 56) cm

Gauge: 24 sts and 32 rows = 4 in / 10 cm in St st on larger needles

Yarn: Kim Dyes Yarn, Tartlet Sport (#2 fine weight; 100% superwash merino; 385 yd / 350 m per 3.5 oz / 100 g): 1 (1, 2, 3) skeins Me Want Cookies

Needles: US 4 (3.5 mm) 16 in / 40 cm circular and dpns, or size needed to obtain gauge; US 3 (3.25 mm) 16 in / 40 cm circular or needles and dpns, or needles one size smaller than needed to obtain gauge

Notions: Tapestry needle, three ½ in / 1.5 cm buttons, six 1 in / 2.5 cm buttons for back flap

Stitch Guide

K1, P1 RIB WORKED FLAT

Row 1: *K1, p1; rep from * to end of row.
Row 2: *P1, k1; rep from * to end of row.
Repeat Rows 1 and 2 for pattern.

K1, P1 RIB IN THE ROUND

Rnd 1: *K1, p1; rep from * to end of rnd.
Repeat Rnd 1 for pattern.

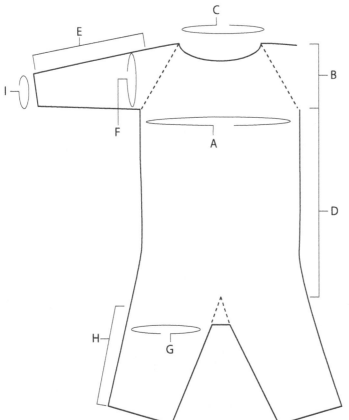

A - 16 (18, 20, 22) in
 40.5 (45.5, 51, 56) cm
B - 3.5 (3.5, 3.75, 4) in
 9 (9, 9.5, 10) cm
C - 7.75 (10, 11.75, 13) in
 19.5 (25.5, 30, 33) cm
D - 10.5 (13.5, 14.5, 15.5) in
 26.5 (34.5, 37, 39.5) cm
E - 7.5 (8.25, 9, 10) in
 19 (21, 23, 25.5) cm
F - 7.5 (7.75, 8.5, 8.75) in
 19 (19.5, 21.5, 22) cm
G - 5.75 (5.75, 6.25, 6.75) in
 14.5 (14.5, 16, 17) cm
H - 5 (6, 7, 8) in
 12.5 (15, 18, 20.5) cm
I - 5.25 (5.5, 6, 6.25) in
 13.5 (14, 15, 16) cm

INSTRUCTIONS

Body

With larger needles, CO 46 (60, 70, 78) sts.

Set-up Row 1 (RS): K4 sts (button band), pm, k5 (9, 11, 13) front sts, pm, k6 (7, 8, 8) sleeve sts, pm, k16 (20, 24, 28) back sts, pm, k6 (7, 8, 8) sleeve sts, pm, k5 (9, 11, 13) front sts, pm, k4 sts (button band).

Set-up Row 2 (WS): K4, purl to last 4 sts, k4 (slipping all markers as you come to them).

Inc Row (RS): K4, sm, (knit to 1 st before m, k1f&b sm, k1f&b) 4 times, knit to end of row—54 (68, 78, 86) sts.

Even Row (WS): K4, purl to last 4 sts, k4 (slipping all markerss as you come to them).

Buttonhole Inc Row (RS): K1, yo, k2tog, k1, sm, (knit to 1st before m, k1f&b, sm, k1f&b) 4 times, knit to end of row—62 (76, 86, 94) sts.

Even Row (WS): K4, purl to last 4 sts, k4 (slipping all markers as you come to them).

Inc Row (RS): K4, sm, (knit to 1 st before m, k1f&b sm, k1f&b) 4 times, knit to end of row—8 sts increased.

Repeat last two rows 3 (3, 4, 4) times more—94 (108, 126, 134) sts.

Work one more WS Even Row.

Buttonhole Inc Row (RS): K1, yo, k2tog, k1, sm, (knit to 1st before m, k1f&b, sm, k1f&b) 4 times, knit to end of row—102 (116, 134, 142) sts.

Even Row (WS): K4, purl to last 4 sts, k4 (slipping all markers as you come to them).

Inc Row (RS): K4, sm, (knit to 1 st before m, k1f&b sm, k1f&b) 4 times, knit to end of row—8 sts increased.

Repeat last two rows 3 (3, 3, 4) times more—134 (148, 166, 182) sts.

Work one more WS Even Row.

Buttonhole Inc Row (RS): K1, yo, k2tog, k1, sm, (knit to 1st before m, k1f&b, sm, k1f&b) 4 times, knit to end of row—142 (156, 174, 190) sts.

Even Row (WS): K4, purl to last 4 sts, k4 (slipping all markers as you come to them).

Inc Row (RS): K4, sm, (knit to 1 st before m, k1f&b sm, k1f&b) 4 times, knit to end of row—150 (164, 182, 198) sts.

Join Fronts and Back (RS): K4, sm, (knit to 1 st before m, k1f&b sm, k1f&b) 4 times, knit to last 4 sts. Slip 4 sts purlwise from the LH needle to spare dpn, then k2tog using 1 st from RH

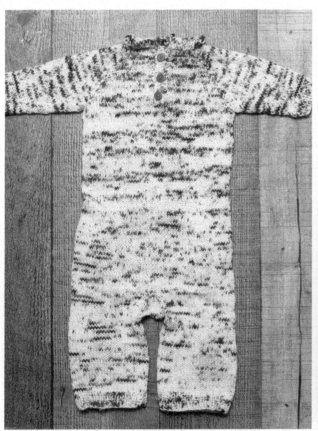

FRONT

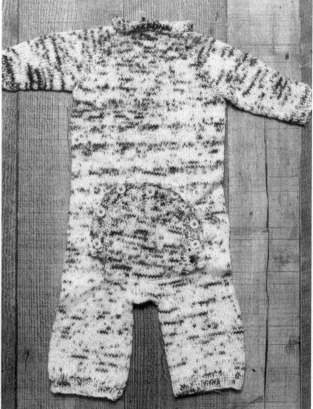

BACK

needle and 1 st from dpn four times—154 (168, 186, 202) sts.

Cut yarn, leaving a 12 in / 30.5 cm tail, slip 19 (23, 26, 29) sts purlwise to the RH needle (all the sts before the first sleeve m).

Separate Sleeves: Remove m, then move 34 (35, 38, 40) sleeve sts to waste yarn, this next m becomes new BOR m, CO 5 sts, knit to next m, remove m, move 34 (35, 38, 40) sleeve sts to waste yarn, remove m, CO 5 sts, knit to end of rnd—96 (108, 120, 132) body sts.

Knit every rnd until piece measures 5 (6, 8, 8) in / 12.5 (15, 20.5, 20.5) cm.

Next Rnd: K17 (17, 19, 20) work in K2, P2 Rib for 20 (24, 26, 30) sts, continue to knit around.

Work in this manner for 1 in. / 2.5 cm.

Then k17 (17, 19, 20), bind off 20 (24, 26, 30) sts in Rib pattern, knit to the end of the rnd.

Work flat in St st for 4 (4.5, 5, 6) in / 10 (11.5, 12.5, 15) cm ending with a WS row.

On the next row, knit to the end of the row, and CO 20 (24, 26, 30) sts.

Knit 4 rnds.

Gusset

Set-up Rnd 1: K 26 (28, 31, 34) sts, place gusset m, k2, place gusset m, k 46 (52, 58, 64) sts, place gusset m, k1, place gusset m, knit to end.

Set-up Rnd 2: Knit.

Gusset Inc Rnd: Knit to gusset m, sm, *m1L, knit to m, m1R, sm; rep from * once, knit to end.

Even Rnd: Knit.

Repeat last 2 rnds four times more, until there are 12 sts between the gusset markers.

Split Legs: Knit to gusset m, move 12 gusset sts to waste yarn, move leg sts to another piece of waste yarn. Then move second set of 12 gusset sts to another piece of waste yarn. Using dpns, pick up and knit 1 st, pm, pick up and knit 1 st and knit the leg sts in the round.

Work in the round until leg measures 4 (5, 6, 7) in / 10 (12.5, 15, 18) cm from split.

Switch to smaller needles and work in K1, P1 Rib for 1 in. / 2.5 cm.

Place sts from second leg on dpns and work as first.

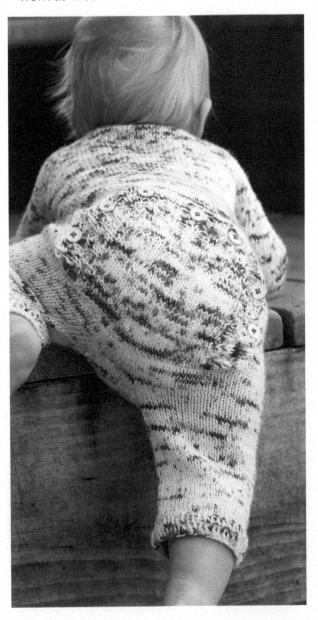

Place gusset sts on separate dpns and use the Kitchener stitch to graft the gusset sts together.

Sleeves

Move 34 (35, 38, 40) sleeve sts to dpns.

Reattach yarn and knit around sleeve sts, pick up and knit 2 sts, pm, pick up and knit 2 sts—38 (39, 42, 44) sts.

Knit 5 rnds.

Dec Rnd: K1, k2tog, knit to last 3 sts before m, ssk, k1—2 sts decreased.

Rep this Dec Rnd every 4th rnd 3 (4, 5, 6) times more.

Work even until sleeve measures 4 (6, 7, 7) in. / 10 (15, 18, 18) cm.

Switch to smaller needles and work K1, P1 Rib for 1 in / 2.5 cm. Bind off all sts in Rib pattern.

Bum Flap

Pick up 24 (26, 28, 30) sts along the bottom, where you cast on the stitches to return to working in the round.

Knit for 4 (4.5, 5, 6) in / 10 (11.5, 12.5, 15) cm, ending with a WS row.

Cut yarn.

Turn piece and pick up 24 (26, 28, 36) sts along right side of flap, knit across 24 (26, 28, 30) sts at the top, pick up 24 (26, 28, 36) sts down the left side of the flap.

Work in K1, P1 Rib for 4 rows.

Buttonhole Row (WS): *P1, k1, yo, k2tog, p1, k1; rep from * to end.

Work K1, P1 Rib for 4 more rows. Bind off in Rib pattern.

NECK EDGING

With smaller needles, starting at the back of the neck, pick up and knit 2 sts for every 3 sts around neck edge.

Work in K1, P1 Rib for 3 rows. Bind off all sts in Rib pattern.

FINISHING

Sew buttons carefully on button band on opposite side matching buttonholes.

Carefully sew buttons opposite buttonholes along bum flap.

Weave in all ends. Wash and block to measurements.

BASIC *Little Glowbug*

This one just might be even easier than the Basic Romper. Worked in a worsted weight, gradient cake yarn, this romper will just fly off your needles. Big stitches, fast knitting—the yarn does all the work for you. This is definitely the pattern you want to reach for when you have a baby shower, say, in a day!

Sizes: Newborn (6 months, 12 months, 18 months)

Finished Chest Circumference: 16 (18, 20, 22) in / 40.5 (45.5, 51, 56) cm

Gauge: 20 sts and 28 rows = 4 in / 10 cm in St st on larger needles

Yarn: Lion Brand Yarn, Crayola Cake Yarn (#4 medium weight; 100% acrylic; 177 yd / 162 m per 3 oz / 85 g): 2 (2, 3, 3) cakes Inchworm

Needles: US 7 (4.5 mm) 16 in / 40 cm circular, or size needed to obtain gauge; US 5 (3.75 mm) 16 in / 40 cm circular and dpn(s), or needles two sizes smaller than size needed to obtain gauge

Notions: Tapestry needle, 1 in / 2.5 cm wide snap tape, sewing needle and thread, waste yarn

Stitch Guide

K1, P1 RIB WORKED FLAT

Row 1: *K1, p1; rep from * to end of row.
Row 2: *P1, k1; rep from * to end of row.
Repeat Rows 1 and 2 for pattern.

K1, P1 RIB IN THE ROUND

Rnd 1: *K1, p1; rep from * to end of rnd.
Repeat Rnd 1 for pattern.

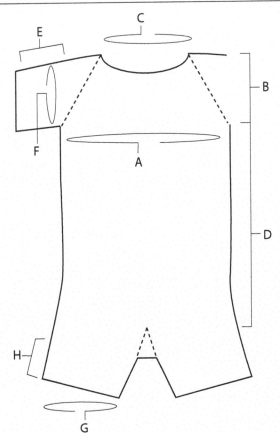

A - 16 (18, 20, 22) in
    40.5 (45.5, 51, 56) cm
B - 3.25 (3.5, 4, 4.25) in
    8.5 (9, 10, 11) cm
C - 9.5 (11, 11.75, 13.5) in
    24 (28, 30, 34.5) cm
D - 10.5 (13.5, 14.5, 15.5) in
    26.5 (34.5, 37, 39.5) cm
E - 2.5 in / 5 cm
F - 6 (6.5, 7.5, 8.25) in
    15 (16.5, 19, 21) cm
G - 9.5 (10.5, 11.5, 12.5) in
    24 (26.5, 29, 32) cm
H - 3.5 (3.5, 4.5, 4.5) in
    9 (9, 11.5, 11.5) cm

INSTRUCTIONS

Body

With larger needles, CO 47 (55, 59, 67) sts.

Set-up Row 1 (RS): K5 sts (button band), pm, k6 (7, 8, 9) front sts, pm, k5 (6, 7, 8) sleeve sts, pm, k15 (19, 19, 23) back sts, pm, k5 (6, 7, 8) sleeve sts, pm, k6 (7, 8, 9) front sts, pm, k5 sts (button band).

Set-up Row 2 (WS): K5, purl to last 5 sts, k5 (slipping all markers as you come to them).

Inc Row (RS): K5, sm, (knit to 1 st before m, k1f&b sm, k1f&b) 4 times, knit to end of row—55 (63, 67, 75) sts.

Even Row (WS): K5, purl to last 5 sts, k5 (slipping all markers as you come to them).

Buttonhole Inc Row (RS): K2, yo, k2tog, k1, sm, (knit to 1st before m, k1f&b, sm, k1f&b) 4 times, knit to end of row—63 (71, 75, 83) sts.

Even Row (WS): K5, purl to last 5 sts, k5 (slipping all markers as you come to them).

Inc Row (RS): K5, sm, (knit to 1 st before m, k1f&b sm, k1f&b) 4 times, knit to end of row—8 sts increased.

Repeat last two rows 2 (3, 4, 4) times more—87 (103, 115, 123) sts.

Work one more WS Even Row.

Buttonhole Inc Row (RS): K2, yo, k2tog, k1, sm, (knit to 1st before m, k1f&b, sm, k1f&b) 4 times, knit to end of row—95 (111, 123, 131) sts.

Even Row (WS): K5, purl to last 5 sts, k5 (slipping all markers as you come to them).

Inc Row (RS): K5, sm, (knit to 1 st before m, k1f&b sm, k1f&b) 4 times, knit to end of row—8 sts increased.

Repeat last two rows 2 (2, 3, 4) times more—119 (135, 155, 171) sts.

Work one more WS Even Row.

Buttonhole Inc Row (RS): K2, yo, k2tog, k1, sm, (knit to 1st before m, k1f&b, sm, k1f&b) 4 times, knit to end of row—127 (143, 163, 179) sts.

Even Row (WS): K5, purl to last 5 sts, k5 (slipping all markers as you come to them).

Join Fronts and Back (RS): K5, sm, (knit to 1 st before m, k1f&b sm, k1f&b) 4 times, knit to last 5 sts. Slip 5 sts purlwise from the LH needle to spare dpn, then k2tog using 1 st from RH needle and 1 st from dpn five times—130 (146, 166, 182) sts.

Knit 1 rnd.

Separate Sleeves: Remove m, then knit to next m, move 27 (30, 35, 38) sleeve sts to waste

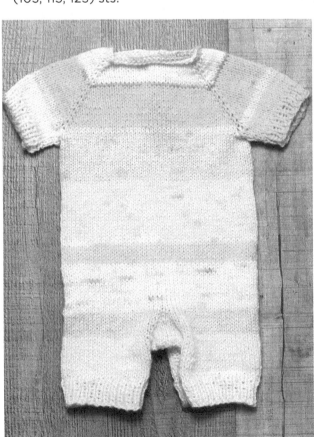

FRONT

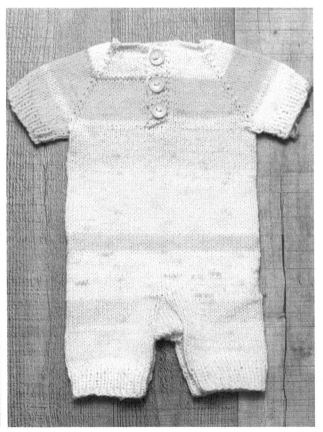

BACK

yarn, CO 1 st, place new BOR m, CO 1 st, remove m, knit to next m, remove m, move 27 (30, 35, 38) sleeve sts to waste yarn, CO 1 st, pm, CO 1 st, knit to end of rnd. Knit every rnd until piece measures 10.5 (13.5, 14.5, 15.5) in / 26.5 (34.5, 37, 39.5) cm from underarm.

Gusset

Set-up Rnd 1: *K19 (22, 24, 27) sts, place gusset m, k1, place gusset m, k39 (44, 49, 54) sts, place gusset m, k1, place gusset m, knit to end.

Set-up Rnd 2: Knit.

Gusset Inc Rnd: Knit to gusset m, sm, *m1L, knit to m, m1R, sm; rep from * once, knit to end.

Even Rnd: Knit.

Repeat last 2 rnds four times more, until there are 11 sts between the gusset markers.

Split Legs: Knit to last gusset m, slip next 11 sts to waste yarn, turn and purl back to back gusset sts, slip next 11 sts to waste yarn. Continue working left leg only in St st flat, until leg measures 2 (2, 3, 3)" [5 (5, 7.5, 7.5) cm] from split.

Note: If preferred here, you can place the right leg sts on waste yarn or a holder, but you can easily leave them on the other portion of the circular needle while working the left leg flat.

Switch to smaller needles and work in k1, p1 rib for 1.5 in / 4 cm.

Gusset Snap Band: With smaller needles and RS facing and starting at the bottom right corner of the front above the Rib stitch, pick up and knit 2 sts for every 3 sts along the leg, move the 11 held gusset sts on to spare needles and knit across, pick up and knit 2 sts for every 3 sts along the leg. Knit every row for 1.5 in / 4 cm. Bind off all sts. Repeat for back side.

Sleeves

Move 27 (30, 35, 38) sleeve sts to dpns.

Reattach yarn and knit around sleeve sts, pick up and knit 2 sts, pm, pick up and knit 1 st—30 (33, 38, 41) sts.

Knit 4 rnds.

Switch to smaller needles and work in K1, P1 Rib for 1.5 in / 4 cm. Bind off all sts in Rib pattern.

NECK EDGING

With smaller needles, starting at the back of the neck, pick up and knit 2 sts for every 3 sts around neck edge.

Work in K1, P1 Rib for 3 rows. Bind off all sts in Rib pattern.

FINISHING

Sew buttons carefully on button band on opposite side matching buttonholes.

Using a sewing machine or needle and thread, carefully sew snap tape along the RS of the gusset snap band.

Weave in all ends. Wash and block to measurements.

RAINBOW STRIPES *Onesie*

Rainbows and babies are simply magical! This is a basic onesie recipe, worked in rainbow stripes for maximum cuteness. You could change out the colors for any palette that makes you smile, or view it as a chance to use up some stash yarn.

Sizes: Newborn (3 months, 6 months, 9 months, 12 months, 18 months)

Finished Chest Circumference: 15 (16, 17, 18, 19, 20) in / 38 (40.5, 43, 45.5, 48.5, 51) cm

Gauge: 20 sts and 28 rows = 4 in / 10 cm in St st on larger needles

Yarn: Knit Picks, Brava Worsted (#4 medium weight; 100% premium acrylic; 54 yd / 50 m per 0.88 oz / 25 g): 1 (1, 1, 1, 1, 2) skeins each of Red (C1), Orange (C2), Canary (C3), Alfafa (C4), Sky (C5), Celestial (C6), Fairy Tale (C7)

Needles: US 6 (4.0 mm) 16 in / 40 cm circular, or size needed to obtain gauge

Notions: Tapestry needle, 1 in / 2.5 cm wide snap tape, sewing needle and thread

STRIPE PATTERN

2 rnds in C1
2 rnds in C2
2 rnds in C3
2 rnds in C4
2 rnds in C5
2 rnds in C6
2 rnds in C7
Stripe pattern is worked throughout pattern in order.

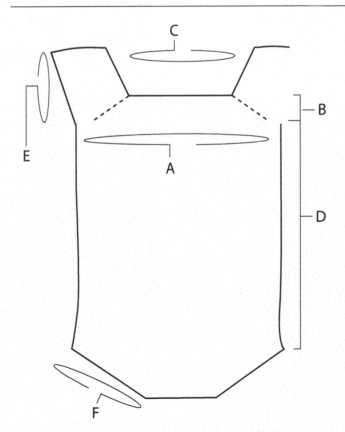

A - 15 (16, 17, 18, 19, 20) in
    38 (40.5, 43, 45.5, 48.5, 51) cm
B - 1.5 (1.5, 1.75, 1.75, 2, 2) in
    4 (4, 4.5, 4.5, 5, 5) cm
C - 13 (13.25, 14.5, 15.5, 15.75, 16.75) in
    33 (33.5, 37, 39.5, 40, 42.5) cm
D - 6 (6.5, 7, 8, 8.5, 9) in
    15 (16.5, 18, 20.5, 21.5, 23) cm
E - 5.25 (5.25, 6, 6.5, 6.75, 7.25) in
    13.5 (13.5, 15, 16.5, 17, 18.5) cm
F - 7.5 (7.25, 8, 8.25, 9.25, 9) in
    19 (18.5, 20.5, 21, 23.5, 23) cm

INSTRUCTIONS

With C1, CO 65 (66, 73, 78, 79, 84) sts, pm, and join to work in the rnd, being careful not to twist your sts.

Set-up Rnd: K16 (16, 18, 20, 20, 22) sleeve sts, pm, k17 (17, 19, 19, 20, 20) back sts, pm, k16 (16, 18, 20, 20, 22) sleeve sts, pm, k16 (17, 18, 19, 19, 20) front sts.

Next Rnd: Knit.

On next rnd switch to C2. Continue the striping pattern as listed above (switching every two rnds).

Inc Rnd: (K1f&b, knit to 1 st before m, k1f&b, sm) 4 times—8 sts increased.

Even Rnd: Knit.

Repeat last two rnds 4 (4, 5, 5, 6, 6) times more—105 (106, 121, 126, 135, 140) sts.

Next Rnd (Create Shoulders): Remove m, bind off 26 (26, 30, 32, 34, 36) sleeve sts, remove m, knit across 27 (27, 31, 31, 34, 34) back sts, remove m, bind off 26 (26, 30, 32, 34, 36) sleeve sts, remove m, then knit across 26 (27, 30, 31, 33, 34) front sts.

Underarm Rnd: CO 6 (6, 6, 7, 7, 8) sts, place new BOR m, CO 5 (7, 6, 7, 7, 8) knit across 27 (27, 31, 31, 34, 34) back sts, bind off 26 (26, 30, 32, 34, 46) sleeve sts, remove m, using the

backwards loop cast-on, CO 11 (13, 12, 14, 14, 16) sts, knit across 26 (27, 30, 31, 33, 34) front sts, knit to end of rnd.

Knit every rnd keeping the stripe pattern as established until piece measures 2 (2.5, 2.5, 3, 3.5, 4) in / 5 (6.5, 6.5, 7.5, 9, 10) cm from underarm.

Inc Rnd: *K4, k1f&b; rep form * to end of rnd—90 (96, 102, 108, 114, 120) sts.

Continue to knit in the rnd until piece measures 6.5 (6.5, 7, 8, 8.5, 9) in / 16.5 (16.5, 18, 20.5, 21.5, 23) cm.

Back Shaping

Row 1 (RS): Bind off 8 (8, 8, 9, 10, 10) sts, k37 (40, 43, 45, 49, 52) sts. Place remaining 45 (48, 51, 54, 57, 60) sts on hold for front.

Row 2 (WS): Bind off 8 (8, 8, 9, 10, 10) sts, purl to end—29 (32, 35, 36, 37, 40) sts.

Work 6 (4, 0, 2, 2, 0) rows in flat St st.

Dec Row (RS): K1, ssk, knit to last 3 sts, k2tog, k1—2 sts decreased.

Even Row (WS): Purl.

Repeat last 2 rows 3 (4, 5, 5, 5, 6) times more—21 (22, 23, 24, 25, 26) sts.

Work in flat St st for 5 (5, 5, 5, 7, 7) rows. Bind off all sts.

FRONT

BACK

Front Shaping

Row 1 (RS): Bind off 10 (10, 12, 12, 14, 14) sts, knit to end.

Row 2 (WS): Bind off 10 (10, 12, 12, 14, 14) sts, purl to end—25 (28, 27, 30, 29, 32) sts.

Work 4 (0, 6, 2, 8, 4) rows in flat St st.

Dec Row (RS): K1, ssk, knit to last 3 sts, k2tog, k1—2 sts decreased.

Even Row (WS): Purl.

Repeat last 2 rows 2 (3, 2, 3, 2, 3) times more— 19 (20, 21, 22, 23, 24) sts. Bind off all sts.

ARM EDGING

With C1, pick up 2 sts for every 3 sts around armhole. Bind off all sts.

NECK EDGING

With C7, pick up sts along neck edging (1 st for every neck st). Bind off all sts.

FINISHING

Weave in all ends. Wash and block as desired. Sew snap tape on opposite sides of bottom flaps.

BAMBOLETTA *Romper*

Because your little one is bound to have a special friend, and what's better than to have them wear a matching romper? Here is a basic pattern to create a romper for your favorite 15 in / 38 cm Waldorf-style doll.

Size: To fit a 15 in / 38 cm Waldorf-style doll

Gauge: 26 sts and 30 rows = 4 in / 10 cm in St st on larger needles

Yarn: Knit Picks, Stroll Tonal (#1 super fine weight; 75% superwash merino wool, 25% nylon; 462 yd / 425 m per 3.5 oz / 100 g): 1 skein Frozen

Needles: US 4 (3.5 mm) 16 in / 40 cm circular and dpns, or size needed to obtain gauge

Notions: Tapestry needle, 1 in / 2.5 cm wide snap tape, sewing needle and thread, waste yarn

Stitch Guide

K1, P1 RIB WORKED FLAT

Row 1: *K1, p1; rep from * to end of row.
Row 2: *P1, k1; rep from * to end of row.
Repeat Rows 1 and 2 for pattern.

K1, P1 IN THE ROUND

Rnd 1: *K1, p1; rep from * to end of rnd.
Repeat Rnd 1 for pattern.

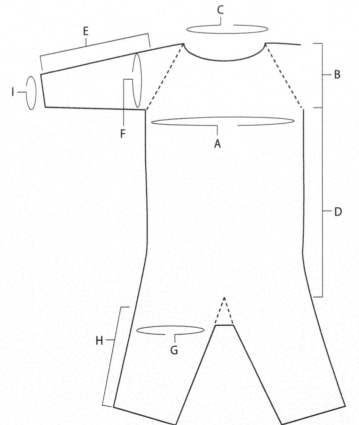

A - 16 in [40.5 cm]

B - 3.75 in [9.5 cm]

C - 9 in [23 cm]

D - 5.5 in [14 cm]

E - 2 in [5 cm]

F - 6 in [15 cm]

G - 8 in [20.5 cm]

H - 3.75 in [9.5 cm]

I - 5.25 in [13.5 cm]

INSTRUCTIONS

Body

With circular needles CO 58 sts as follows: CO 4 (snap band), pm, CO 8 (back), pm, CO 7 (sleeve), pm, CO 20 (front), pm, CO 7 (sleeve), pm, CO 8 (back), pm, CO 4 (snap band).

Set-up Row 1 (RS): K4, work in k1, p1 rib to last 4 sts, k4.

Set-up Row 2 (WS): K4, work in k1, p1 rib to last 4 sts, k4.

Inc Row (RS): K4, sm, (knit to 1 st before m, k1f&b sm, k1f&b) 4 times, knit to end of row—66 sts.

Even Row (WS): K4, purl to last 4 sts, k4 (slipping all markers as you come to them).

Repeat last two rows 13 times more—170 sts.

Work one more WS Even Row.

Join Fronts and Back (RS): K4, sm, (knit to 1 st before m, k1f&b sm, k1f&b) 4 times, knit to last 4 sts. Slip 4 sts purlwise from the LH needle to spare dpn, then k2tog using 1 st from the RH needle and 1 st from dpn four times—174 sts.

Separate Sleeves: Knit to next m, remove m, then move 37 sleeve sts to waste yarn, remove m, CO 1 st, place new BOR m, CO 1 st, knit to next m, remove m, move 37 sleeve sts to waste yarn, CO 2 sts, knit to end of rnd. Knit every rnd until piece measures 5.5 in / 14 cm from underarm.

Gusset

Set-up Rnd 1: K26, place gusset m, M1R, place gusset m, k52, place gusset m, M1R, place gusset m, knit to end.

Set-up Rnd 2: Knit.

Gusset Inc Rnd: (Knit to gusset m, sm, M1L, knit to gusset m, m1R, sm) twice, knit to end.

Even Rnd: Knit.

Repeat last 2 rnds twice more, until there are 7 sts between the gusset markers.

Split Legs: Knit to gusset m, move 7 gusset sts to waste yarn, move leg sts to another piece of waste yarn. Then move second set of 7 gusset sts to another piece of waste yarn. Using dpns, knit the first set of leg sts in the round.

Work in the round until leg measures 3 in / 7.5 cm from split.

Work in K1, P1 Rib for 4 rnds. Bind off all sts in Rib pattern.

Place sts from second leg on dpns and work as first.

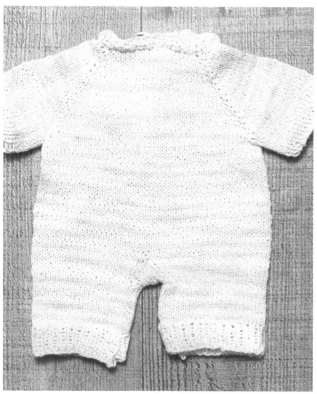

FRONT

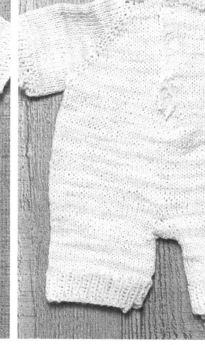

BACK

Place gusset sts on separate dpns and use the Kitchener stitch to graft the gusset sts together.

Sleeves

Move 37 sleeve sts to dpns.

Reattach yarn and knit around sleeve sts, pick up and knit 1 st, pm, pick up and knit 1 st—39 sts. Knit 2 rnds.

Dec Rnd: K1, k2tog, knit to last 3 sts before m, ssk, k1—37 sts.

Even Rnd: Knit.

Repeat last two rnds once more—35 sts.

Final Dec Rnd: K1, k2tog, knit to end—34 sts.

Work in K1, P1 Rib for 4 rnds. Bind off all sts in Rib pattern.

FINISHING

Weave in all ends.
Sew snap tape on back neck band.
Wash and block to measurements.

FUN ON THE *Farm*

Sheep

A book of knitting patterns including animal themes has to have a baby sheep, doesn't it? The sheep is one of my favorite farm animals, and I'm sure it's one of yours as well. This one can be super fun in a squishy pale cream yarn, but it would be equally adorable as a rainbow sheep, or even a green sheep (has anybody else had to read Mem Fox's *Where Is the Green Sheep?* over and over to their children? Definitely a favorite!). *Baa* says the sheep!

Sizes: Newborn (6 months, 12 months, 18 months)

Finished Chest Circumference: 16 (18, 20, 22) in / 40.5 (45.5, 51, 56) cm

Finished Head Circumference: 10.5 (12, 13.25, 14.5) in / 26.5 (30.5, 33.5, 37) cm

Gauge: 24 sts and 32 rows = 4 in / 10 cm in St st on larger needles

Yarn: Jilly and Kiddles, Ideal DK (#3 light weight; 75% superwash merino, 25% nylon; 246 yd / 225 m per 3.5 oz / 100 g): 2 (2, 3, 3) skeins in Low Fat Milk

Needles: US 6 (4.0 mm) 16 in / 40 cm circular, or size needed to obtain gauge; US 4 (3.5 mm) 16 in / 40 cm circular and dpn(s), or needles two sizes smaller than size needed to obtain gauge

Notions: Tapestry needle, three ½ in / 1.5 cm JHB buttons, 1 in / 2.5 cm wide snap tape, sewing needle and thread, waste yarn

Stitch Guide

K1, P1 RIB WORKED FLAT

Row 1: *K1, p1; rep from * to end of row.
Row 2: *P1, k1; rep from * to end of row.
Repeat Rows 1 and 2 for pattern.

K1, P1 RIB IN THE ROUND

Rnd 1: *K1, p1; rep from * to end of rnd.
Repeat Rnd 1 for pattern.

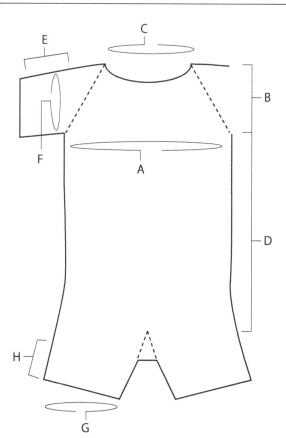

A - 16 (18, 20, 22) in
   40.5 (45.5, 51, 56) cm
B - 3.75 (4.25, 4.25, 4.5) in
   9.5 (11, 11, 11.5) cm
C - 7.75 (8.5, 9.5, 10.5) in
   19.5 (21.5, 24, 26.5) cm
D - 10.5 (13.5, 14.5, 15.5) in
   26.5 (34.5, 37, 39.5) cm
E - 1.5 (1.5, 1.25, 1.5) in
   4 (4, 3, 4) cm
F - 6 (6.75, 7, 7.25) in
   15 (17, 18, 18.5) cm
G - 9.25 (10.25, 10.75, 11.25) in
   23.5 (26, 27.5, 28.5) cm
H - 3 (3.5, 3.75, 4) in
   7.5 (9, 9.5, 10) cm

INSTRUCTIONS

Body

With smaller needles, CO 47 (51, 57, 63) sts.

Set-up Row 1 (RS): K11 (11, 13, 13) front sts, pm, k6 (6, 6, 8) sleeve sts, pm, k16 (20, 22, 24) back sts, pm, k6 (6, 6, 8) sleeve sts, pm, k8 (8, 10, 10) front sts.

Set-up Row 2 (WS): Knit.

Set-up Row 3: Knit.

Buttonhole Row (WS): Knit to last 3 sts, k2tog, yo, k1.

Switch to larger needles and MC.

Inc Row (RS): (Knit to 1 st before m, k1f&b, sm, k1f&b) 4 times, knit to end—55 (59, 65, 71) sts.

Even Row (WS): K3, purl to last 3 sts, k3 (slipping all markers as you come to them).

Next Inc Row (RS): (Knit to 1 st before m, k1f&b, sm, k1f&b) 4 times, knit to end—63 (67, 73, 79) sts.

Buttonhole Row (WS): K3, purl to last 3 sts, k2tog, yo, k1.

Next Inc Row (RS): (Knit to 1 st before m, k1f&b, sm, k1f&b) 4 times, knit to end—71 (75, 81, 87) sts.

Row 8: K3, purl to last 3 sts, k3.

Joining Rnd (RS): Slip 3 sts purlwise from the RH needle to spare dpn, then k2tog using 1 st from RH needle and 1 st from dpn three times. Join to work in the round and place a different type of marker to distinguish the start of the round, (knit to 1 st before m, k1f&b, sm, k1f&b) 4 times, knit to end of rnd—76 (80, 86, 92) sts.

Even Rnd: Knit.

Inc Rnd: (Knit to 1 st before m, k1f&b, sm, k1f&b) 4 times, knit to end—84 (88, 94, 100) sts.

Repeat last 2 rnds 10 (12, 12, 13) times—164 (184, 190, 204) sts.

Separate Sleeves: Knit to 1st m, remove m, slip 36 (40, 40, 44) sleeve sts to waste yarn, CO 2 sts, remove m, knit to next marker, remove m, slip 36 (40, 40, 44) sleeve sts to waste yarn, CO 2 sts, remove m, knit to end of rnd—96 (108, 114, 120) sts.

Knit even until piece measures 10.5 (13.5, 14.5, 15.5) in / 26.5 (34.5, 37, 39.5) cm from underarm.

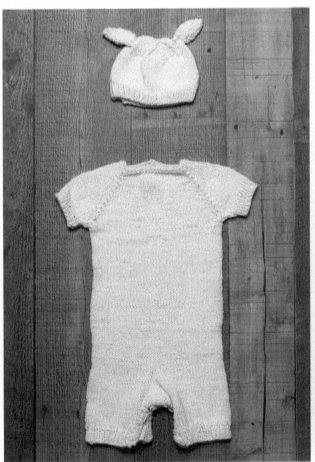

FRONT

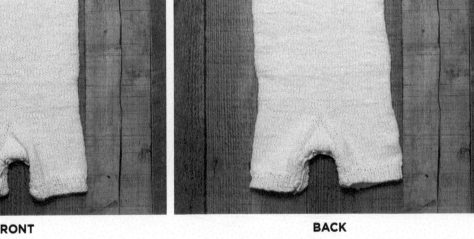

BACK

Gusset

Set-up Rnd: K1, place gusset marker, k46 (52, 55, 58), place gusset marker, k2, place gusset marker, knit to 1 st before BOR, place gusset marker, k1.

Inc Rnd: Knit to gusset m, m1L, sm, knit to next gusset m, sm, m1R, knit to next gusset m, M1L, sm, knit to next gusset m, sm, M1R, knit to end.
Repeat last 2 rnds until there are 11 sts between each set of gusset markers.

Split Legs: Knit to last gm, slip next 11 sts to waste yarn, turn and purl back to the back gusset sts, slip next 11 sts to waste yarn. Continue working left leg only in St st flat, until leg measures 2 (2.5, 2.75, 3) in / 5 (6.5, 7, 7.5) cm from split.

Note: If preferred here, you can place the right leg sts on waste yarn or a holder, but you can easily leave them on the other portion of the circular needle while working the left leg flat.

Change to smaller needles and work K1, P1 Rib for 1 in / 2.5 cm. Bind off in Rib pattern.
Repeat for second leg.

Gusset Snap Band: With smaller needles and the RS of the romper front facing, start at the bottom right corner, and pick up and knit 2 sts for every 3 rows along the leg, move the 11 held sts onto spare needles and knit across, pick up and knit 2 sts for every 3 rows down left side. Knit every row for 1.5 in / 4 cm. Bind off in Rib pattern. Repeat for back side.

Sleeves

Move 36 (40, 40, 44) sleeve sts to dpn(s). Knit around sleeve sts, pick up and knit 2 sts, pm, pick up and knit 2 sts. Knit 3 rnds.

Dec Rnd: K1, k2tog, knit to last 3 sts before m, ssk, k1—2 sts decreased.

Even Rnd: Knit.

Rep Dec Rnd 1 (1, 0, 1) time more—36 (40, 42, 44) sts.

Switch to smaller needles and work in K1, P1 Rib in the round for 3 rnds.

Bind off in Rib pattern.

FINISHING

Sew buttons carefully on button band on opposite side matching buttonholes.

Using a sewing machine or needle and thread, carefully sew snap tape along RS of the gusset snap band.

Weave in all ends. Wash and block to measurements.

Hat

With smaller needles, CO 64 (72, 80, 88) sts. Place marker and join to work in the round, being careful not to twist your sts.

Work K1, P1 Rib for 1 in / 2.5 cm.

Knit 5 rnds.

Switch to larger needles and knit until hat
   measures 3.5 (3.5, 4, 5) in / 9 (9, 10, 12.5) cm
   from cast-on edge.
Dec Rnd: *K6, k2tog; repeat from * to end of
   rnd—56 (63, 70, 77) sts.
Knit 1 rnd.
Dec Rnd: *K5, k2tog; repeat from * to end of
   rnd—48 (54, 60, 66) sts.
Knit 2 rnds.
Dec Rnd: *K4, k2tog; repeat from * to end of
   rnd—40 (45, 50, 55) sts.
Knit 1 rnd.
Dec Rnd: *K3, k2tog; repeat from * to end of
   rnd—32 (36, 40, 44) sts.
Dec Rnd: *K2, k2tog; repeat from * to end of
   rnd—24 (27, 30, 33) sts.
Dec Rnd: K0 (1, 0, 1) *k2tog, repeat from * to
   end of rnd—12 (14, 15, 17) sts.
Dec Rnd: K0 (0, 1, 1), *k2tog, repeat from * to
   end of rnd—6 (7, 8, 9) sts.
Cut yarn leaving a 12 in / 30.5 cm tail. Weave
   tail through all remaining sts and pull
   tight to close.

Ears (make 2)

OUTER EAR (MAKE 2)
CO 6 sts.
Row 1: Knit.
Row 2: Purl.
Rows 3 and 4: Repeat Rows 1 and 2.
Row 5: K1f&b, knit to last st, K1f&b—2 sts
   increased.
Row 6: Purl.
Rows 7-10: Repeat Rows 1 and 2.
Row 11: K2tog, knit to last 2 sts, ssk—2 sts
   decreased.
Row 12: Purl.
Row 13: K2tog, k2, ssk—2 sts decreased.
Row 14: Purl.
Row 15: K2tog, ssk—2 sts decreased.
Row 16: P2tog—1 st rem.
Cut yarn leaving a 12 in / 30.5 cm tail and pull
   through remaining st.

INNER EAR (MAKE 2)
CO 4 sts.
Row 1: Knit.
Row 2: Purl.
Rows 3 and 4: Repeat Rows 1 and 2.
Row 5: K1f&b, knit to last st, k1f&b—2 sts
   increased.
Row 6: Purl.
Rows 7-10: Repeat Rows 1 and 2.
Row 11: K2tog, knit to last 2 sts, ssk—2 sts
   decreased.
Row 12: Purl.
Row 13: K2tog, ssk—2 sts decreased.
Row 14: Purl.
Row 15: K2tog—1 st rem.
Cut yarn leaving a 12 in / 30.5 cm tail and pull
   remaining st through it.

ASSEMBLY
Put the two sides of the ear together with WS
   facing, and whipstich together. Using the
   photo as a guide, sew each ear to one side
   of the hat toward the front. (Hint: It is helpful
   to try the hat on a baby and mark where you
   would like to have the ears placed.)

FINISHING

Weave in all ends. Wash and block to
   measurements.

Pig

This is another
one that was inspired
by one of our favorite books.
Charlotte's Web, anyone? Well,
that and endless rounds of "This
Little Piggy," and then there was
that Peppa phase that my youngest
daughter went through for what felt like
forever (although, what is cuter than
a pig with the most polite British
accent you ever heard?). Whatever
piggy strikes your fancy, this
one is sure to have you
tickled pink!

Sizes: Newborn (6 months, 12 months, 18 months)

Finished Chest Circumference: 16 (18, 20, 22) in / 40.5 (45.5, 51, 56) cm

Finished Head Circumference: 10.5 (12, 13.25, 14.5) in / 26.5 (30.5, 33.5, 37) cm

Gauge: 20 sts and 28 rows = 4 in / 10 cm in St st on larger needles

Yarn: Camellia Fiber Co., Merino Worsted (#4 medium weight; 100% merino; 215 yd / 195 m per 3.5 oz / 100 g): 2 (2, 3, 3) skeins Camellia

Needles: US 7 (4.5 mm) 16 in / 40 cm circular, or size needed to obtain gauge; US 5 (3.75 mm), 16 in / 40 cm circular and dpn(s), or needles two sizes smaller than size needed to obtain gauge

Notions: Tapestry needle, 1 in / 2.5 cm wide snap tape, sewing needle and thread, waste yarn

Stitch Guide

K1, P1 RIB WORKED FLAT

Row 1: *K1, p1; rep from * to end of row.
Row 2: *P1, k1; rep from * to end of row.
Repeat Rows 1 and 2 for attern.

K1, P1 RIB IN THE ROUND

Rnd 1: *K1, p1; rep from * to end of rnd.
Repeat Rnd 1 for pattern.

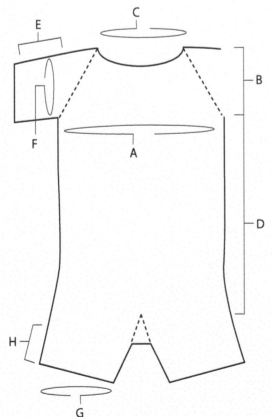

A - 16 (18, 20, 22) in
40.5 (45.5, 51, 56) cm
B - 3.25 (3.5, 4, 4.25) in
8.5 (9, 10, 11) cm
C - 9.5 (11, 11.75, 13.5) in
24 (28, 30, 34.5) cm
D - 10.5 (13.5, 14.5, 15.5) in
26.5 (34.5, 37, 39.5) cm
E - 2.5 in / 5 cm
F - 6 (6.5, 7.5, 8.25) in
15 (16.5, 19, 21) cm
G - 9.5 (10.5, 11.5, 12.5) in
24 (26.5, 29, 32) cm
H - 3.5 (3.5, 4.5, 4.5) in
9 (9, 11.5, 11.5) cm

INSTRUCTIONS

Body

With larger needles, CO 47 (55, 59, 67) sts.

Set-up Row 1 (RS): K5 sts (button band), pm, k6 (7, 8, 9) front sts, pm, k5 (6, 7, 8) sleeve sts, pm, k15 (19, 19, 23) back sts, pm, k5 (6, 7, 8) sleeve sts, pm, k6 (7, 8, 9) front sts, pm, k5 sts (button band).

Set-up Row 2 (WS): K5, purl to last 5 sts, k5 (slipping all markers as you come to them).

Inc Row (RS): K5, sm, (knit to 1 st before m, k1f&b sm, k1f&b) 4 times, knit to end of row—55 (63, 67, 75) sts.

Even Row (WS): K5, purl to last 5 sts, k5 (slipping all markers as you come to them).

Buttonhole Inc Row (RS): K2, yo, k2tog, k1, sm, (knit to 1st before m, k1f&b, sm, k1f&b) 4 times, knit to end of row—63 (71, 75, 83) sts.

Even Row (WS): K5, purl to last 5 sts, k5 (slipping all markers as you come to them).

Inc Row (RS): K5, sm, (knit to 1 st before m, k1f&b sm, k1f&b) 4 times, knit to end of row—8 sts increased.

Repeat last two rows 2 (3, 4, 4) times more—87 (103, 115, 123) sts.

Work one more WS Even Row.

Buttonhole Inc Row (RS): K2, yo, k2tog, k1, sm, (knit to 1st before m, k1f&b, sm, k1f&b) 4 times, knit to end of row—95 (111, 123, 131) sts.

Even Row (WS): K5, purl to last 5 sts, k5 (slipping all markers as you come to them).

Inc Row (RS): K5, sm, (knit to 1 st before m, k1f&b sm, k1f&b) 4 times, knit to end of row—8 sts increased.

Repeat last two rows 2 (2, 3, 4) times more—119 (135, 155, 171) sts.

Work one more WS Even Row.

Buttonhole Inc Row (RS): K2, yo, k2tog, k1, sm, (knit to 1st before m, k1f&b, sm, k1f&b) 4 times, knit to end of row—127 (143, 163, 179) sts.

Even Row (WS): K5, purl to last 5 sts, k5 (slipping all markers as you come to them).

Join Fronts and Back (RS): K5, sm, (knit to 1 st before m, k1f&b sm, k1f&b) 4 times, knit to last 5 sts. Slip 5 sts purlwise from the LH needle to spare dpn, then k2tog using 1 st from RH needle and 1 st from dpn five times—130 (146, 166, 182) sts.

Knit 1 rnd.

Separate Sleeves: Remove m, then knit to next m, move 27 (30, 35, 38) sleeve sts to waste

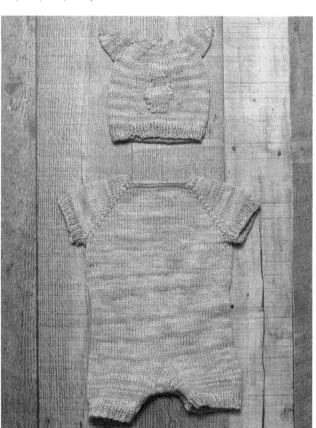

FRONT

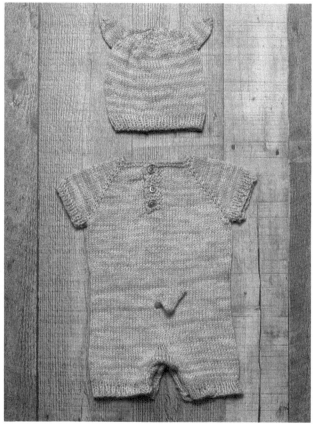

BACK

yarn, CO 1 st, place new BOR m, CO 1 st, remove m, knit to next m, remove m, move 27 (30, 35, 38) sleeve sts to waste yarn, CO 1 st, pm, CO 1 st, knit to end of rnd.
Knit every rnd until piece measures 10.5 (13.5, 14.5, 15.5) in / 26.5 (34.5, 37, 39.5) cm from underarm.

Gusset

Set-up Rnd 1: K19 (22, 24, 27) sts, place gusset m, k1, place gusset m, k39 (44, 49, 54) sts, place gusset m, k1, place gusset m, knit to end.

Set-up Rnd 2: Knit.

Gusset Inc Rnd: Knit to gusset m, sm, *m1L, knit to m, m1R, sm; rep from * once, knit to end.

Even Rnd: Knit.
Repeat last 2 rnds four times more, until there are 11 sts between the gusset markers.

Split Legs: Knit to last gusset m, slip next 11 sts to waste yarn, turn and purl back to the back gusset sts, slip next 11 sts to waste yarn. Continue working left leg only in St st flat, until leg measures 2 (2, 3, 3) in / 5 (5, 7.5, 7.5) cm from split.

Note: If preferred here, you can place the right leg sts on waste yarn or a holder, but you can easily leave them on the other portion of the circular needle while working the left leg flat.

Switch to smaller needles and work in K1, P1 Rib for 1.5 in / 4 cm.

Gusset Snap Band: With smaller needles and RS facing and starting at the bottom right corner of the front above the Rib stitch, pick up and knit 2 sts for every 3 sts along the leg, move the 11 held gusset sts on to spare needles and knit across, pick up and knit 2 sts for every 3 sts along the leg. Knit every row for 1.5 in / 4 cm. Bind off all sts. Repeat for back side.

Sleeves

Move 27 (30, 35, 38) sleeve sts to dpns.

Reattach yarn and knit around sleeve sts, pick up and knit 2 sts, pm, pick up and knit 1 st—30 (33, 38, 41) sts.

Knit 4 rnds.

Switch to smaller needles and work in K1, P1 Rib for 1.5 in / 4 cm.

NECK EDGING

With smaller needles, starting at the back of the neck, pick up and knit 2 sts for every 3 sts around neck edge.

Work in K1, P1 Rib for 3 rows. Bind off all sts in Rib pattern.

Tail

With dpn(s), CO 3 sts. *Knit the 3 sts across the dpn, from the left needle to the right needle. Then, slide the sts from one end of the needle to the other, while holding the tail in back, repeat from * until I-cord is 5 in / 12.5 cm. Bind off all sts.

Sew tail to the back, about 3 in / 7.5 cm above the start of the gusset. Gently curl tail around your finger or a spare dpn.

FINISHING

Sew buttons carefully on button band on opposite side matching buttonholes.

Using a sewing machine or needle and thread, carefully sew snap tape along the RS of the gusset snap band. Weave in all ends. Wash and block to measurements.

Hat

With larger needles, cast on 56 (64, 72, 80) sts, place marker and join in the round, being careful not to twist stitches.

Rnds 1–8: Work K1, P1 Rib.

Knit for 5.5 in / 14 cm.

CROWN SHAPING

Switch to dpn(s) when necessary.

Rnd 1: *K6, k2tog; repeat from * around—49 (56, 63, 70) sts.

Rnds 2–4: Knit.

Rnd 5: *K5, k2tog; repeat from * around—42 (48, 54, 60) sts.

Rnds 6–7: Knit.

Rnd 8: *K4, k2tog; repeat from * around—35 (40, 45, 50) sts.

Rnd 9: Knit.

Rnd 10: *K3, k2tog; repeat from * around—28 (32, 36, 40) sts.

Rnd 11: *K2, k2tog; repeat from * around—21 (24, 27, 30) sts.

Rnd 12: Knit.

Rnd 13: *K1, k2tog; repeat from * around—14 (16, 18, 20) sts.

Rnd 14: *K2tog; repeat from * around—7 (8, 9, 10) sts.

Cut yarn and thread through remaining live stitches. Pull tightly and secure. Weave in all loose ends.

EARS (MAKE 2)

Using dpn(s) CO 16 sts, pm and join to work in the rnds.

Knit 6 rnds.

Dec Rnd: *Ssk, k4, k2tog; rep from * once—12 sts.

Knit 1 rnd.

Dec Rnd: *Ssk, k2, k2tog; rep from * once—8 sts.

Dec Rnd: *Ssk, k2tog; rep from * once—4 sts.

Dec Rnd: K2tog twice—2 sts.

K2tog, cut yarn and pull tight through remaining st.

Sew ears on opposite sides of the hat, using photos as a guide.

NOSE

CO 3 sts.

WS: Purl

RS Inc Row: K1f&b, k1, k1f&b—5 sts.

WS: Purl

RS Inc Row: K1f&b, k3, k1f&b—7 sts.

WS: Purl.

RS Inc Row: K1f&b, k5, k1f&b—9 sts.

WS: Purl.

RS: Knit.

WS: Purl.

RS Dec Row: Ssk, k5, k2tog—7 sts.

WS: Purl.

RS Dec Row: Ssk, k3, k2tog—5 sts.

WS: Purl.

RS Dec Row: Ssk, k1, k2tog—3 sts.

WS: Purl

Bind off all sts.

Sew nose to the middle front of the hat, using photos as a guide.

FINISHING

Weave in all ends. Wash and block hat to measurements.

Frog

Ribbit! Ribbit! If you hop to it real quick, you'll have a fun frog on your hands in no time at all! The yarn used is absolutely perfect for playtime—it's cozy, easy to clean, and super soft to knit. The best part? The fun eyes that sit right on top of the hood! This one sure packs a punch, so don't wait, hop right to it!

Sizes: Newborn (6 months, 12 months, 18 months)

Finished Chest Circumference: 16 (18, 20, 22) in / 40.5 (45.5, 51, 56) cm

Gauge: 24 sts and 32 rows = 4 in / 10 cm in St st on larger needles

Yarn: Knit One Crochet Too, DungarEASE (#4 medium weight; 60% cotton, 40% acrylic; 250 yd / 228 m per 3.5 oz / 100 g): 1 (1, 2, 2) skeins #538 Cactus (MC) and 1 (1, 1, 1) skeins #282 Rose Shadow (C1), scrap yarn in white and black for eyes

Needles: US 4 (3.5 mm), 16 in / 40 cm circulars and dpns, or size needed to obtain gauge; US 3 (3.25 mm), 16 in / 40 cm circular and dpns, or needles one size smaller than needed to obtain gauge

Notions: Tapestry needle, three ½ in / 1.5 cm JHB buttons, six 1 in / 2.5 cm buttons for back flap

Stitch Guide

K1, P1 RIB WORKED FLAT

Row 1: *K1, p1; rep from * to end of row.
Row 2: *P1, k1; rep from * to end of row.
Repeat Rows 1 and 2 for pattern.

K1, P1 RIB IN THE ROUND

Rnd 1: *K1, p1; rep from * to end of rnd.
Repeat Rnd 1 for pattern.

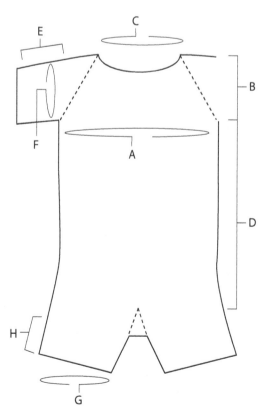

A - 16 (18, 20, 22) in
  40.5 (45.5, 51, 56) cm
B - 3.25 (3.5, 4, 4.25) in
  8.5 (9, 10, 11) cm
C - 9.5 (11, 11.75, 13.5) in
  24 (28, 30, 34.5) cm
D - 10.5 (13.5, 14.5, 15.5) in
  26.5 (34.5, 37, 39.5) cm
E - 2.5 in / 5 cm
F - 6 (6.5, 7.5, 8.25) in
  15 (16.5, 19, 21) cm
G - 9.5 (10.5, 11.5, 12.5) in
  24 (26.5, 29, 32) cm
H - 4 (4, 5, 6) in
  10 (10, 13, 15) cm

INSTRUCTIONS

Body

With larger needles and MC, provisionally CO 46 (60, 70, 78) sts.

Set-up Row 1 (RS): K4 sts (button band), k5 (9, 11, 13) front sts, pm, k6 (7, 8, 8) sleeve sts, pm, k16 (20, 24, 28) back sts, pm, k6 (7, 8, 8) sleeve sts, pm, k5 (9, 11, 13) front sts, pm, k4 sts (button band).

Set-up Row 2 (WS): K4, purl to last 4 sts, k4 (slipping all markers as you come to them).

Inc Row (RS): K4, sm, (knit to 1 st before m, k1f&b sm, k1f&b) 4 times, knit to end of row—54 (68, 78, 86) sts.

Even Row (WS): K4, purl to last 4 sts, k4 (slipping all markers as you come to them).

Buttonhole Inc Row (RS): K1, yo, k2tog, k1, sm, (knit to 1st before m, k1f&b, sm, k1f&b) 4 times, knit to end of row—62 (76, 86, 94) sts.

Even Row (WS): K4, purl to last 4 sts, k4 (slipping all markers as you come to them).

Inc Row (RS): K4, sm, (knit to 1 st before m, k1f&b sm, k1f&b) 4 times, knit to end of row—8 sts increased.

Repeat last two rows 3 (3, 4, 4) times more—94 (108, 126, 134) sts.

Then work one more WS Even Row.

Buttonhole Inc Row (RS): K1, yo, k2tog, k1, sm, (knit to 1st before m, k1f&b, sm, k1f&b) 4 times, knit to end of row—102 (116, 134, 142) sts.

Even Row (WS): K4, purl to last 4 sts, k4 (slipping all markers as you come to them).

Inc Row (RS): K4, sm, (knit to 1 st before m, k1f&b sm, k1f&b) 4 times, knit to end of row—8 sts increased.

Repeat last two rows 3 (3, 3, 4) times more—134 (148, 166, 182) sts.

Then work one more WS Even Row.

Buttonhole Inc Row (RS): K1, yo, k2tog, k1, sm, (knit to 1st before m, k1f&b, sm, k1f&b) 4 times, knit to end of row—142 (156, 174, 190) sts.

Even Row (WS): K4, purl to last 4 sts, k4 (slipping all markers as you come to them).

Inc Row (RS): K4, sm, (knit to 1 st before m, k1f&b sm, k1f&b) 4 times, knit to end of row—150 (164, 182, 198) sts.

Join Fronts and Back (RS): K4, sm, (knit to 1 st before m, k1f&b sm, k1f&b) 4 times, knit to last 4 sts. Slip 4 sts purlwise from the LH needle

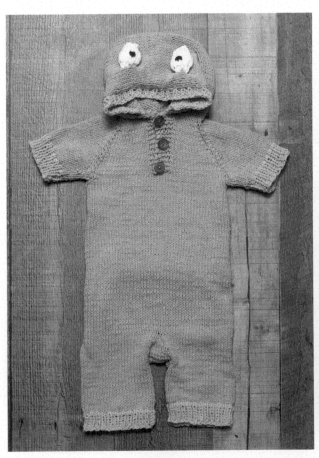

FRONT

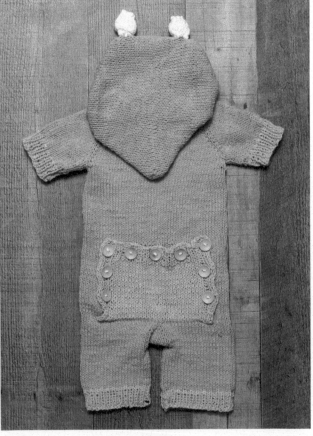

BACK

to spare dpn, then k2tog using 1 st from the RH needle and 1 st from dpn four times—154 (168, 186, 202) sts.

Cut yarn, leaving a 12 in / 30.5 cm tail, slip 19 (23, 26, 29) sts purlwise to RH needle (all the sts before the first sleeve m).

Separate Sleeves: Remove m, then move 34 (35, 38, 40) sleeve sts to waste yarn, this next m becomes new BOR m, CO 5 sts, knit to next m, remove m, move 34 (35, 38, 40) sleeve sts to waste yarn, remove m, CO 5 sts, knit to end of rnd—96 (108, 120, 132) body sts.

Knit every rnd until piece measures 5 (6, 8, 8) in / 12.5 (15, 20.5, 20.5) cm.

Next Rnd: K17 (17, 19, 20) work in K2, P2 Rib for 20 (24, 26, 30) sts, continue to knit around.

Work in this manner for 1 in / 2.5 cm.

Then k17 (17, 19, 20), bind off 20 (24, 26, 30) sts in Rib pattern, knit to the end of the rnd.

Work flat in St st for 4 (4.5, 5, 6) in / 10 (11.5, 12.5, 15) cm, ending with a WS row.

On the next row, knit to the end of the row, and CO 20 (24, 26, 30) sts.

Knit 4 rnds.

Gusset

Set-up Rnd 1: K26 (28, 31, 34) sts, place gusset m, k2, place gusset m, k 46 (52, 58, 64) sts, place gusset m, k1, place gusset m, knit to end.

Set-up Rnd 2: Knit.

Gusset Inc Rnd: Knit to gusset m, sm, *m1L, knit to m, m1R, sm; rep from * once, knit to end.

Even Rnd: Knit.

Repeat last 2 rnds four times more, until there are 12 sts between the gusset markers.

Split Legs: Knit to gusset m, move 12 gusset sts to waste yarn, move leg sts to another piece of waste yarn. Then move second set of 12 gusset sts to another piece of waste yarn. Using dpns, pick up and knit 1 st, pm, pick up and knit 1 st and knit the leg sts in the round.

Work in the round until leg measures 3 (3, 4, 5) in / 7.5 (7.5, 10, 12.5) cm from split

Switch to smaller needles and CC, work in K1, P1 Rib for 1 in / 2.5 cm.

Place sts from second leg on dpns and work as first.

Place gusset sts on separate dpns and use the Kitchener stitch to graft the gusset sts together.

Sleeves

Move 34 (35, 38, 40) sleeve sts to dpns.
Reattach yarn and knit around sleeve sts, pick up and knit 2 sts, pm, pick up and knit 2 sts—38 (39, 42, 44) sts.
Knit 5 rnds.
Dec Rnd: K1, k2tog, knit to last 3 sts before m, ssk, k1—2 sts decreased.
Rep this Dec Rnd every 4th rnd twice more.
Switch to smaller needles and CC, work K1, P1 Rib for 1 in / 2.5 cm. Bind off all sts in Rib pattern.

Flap

With CC, pick up 24 (26, 28, 30) sts.
Knit for 4 (4.5, 5, 6) in / 10 (11.5, 12.5, 15) cm, ending with a WS row. Cut yarn.
Turn piece and pick up 24 (26, 28, 36) sts along right side of flap, knit across 24 (26, 28, 30) sts at the top, pick up 24 (26, 28, 36) sts down the left side of the flap.
Work in K1, P1 Rib for 4 rows.
Buttonhole Row (WS): *P1, k1, yo, k2tog, p1, k1; rep from * to end.
Work K1, P1 Rib for 4 more rows. Bind off in Rib pattern.

Hood

With MC, carefully undo provisional CO and place sts on larger needles.
Next Row (WS): Purl.
Inc Row 1 (RS): K1 (6, 11, 12), *k1, k1f&b; rep from * to last 1 (6, 11, 12) sts—66 (72, 72, 81) sts.
Next Row: Purl.
Inc Row 2: *K2, k1f&b; rep from * to end of row—88 (96, 96, 108) sts.
Work in St st until hood measures 7 (7, 7.5, 8) in / 18 (18, 19, 20.5) cm.
Using Kitchener stitch graft hood closed.

HOOD EDGING

With smaller needles and CC, beginning at right front edge after the button band, pick up and knit 2 sts for every 3 sts around the fronts, the hood, and the left front.
Work in K1, P1 Rib for 3 rows. Bind off in Rib pattern.

Eyes (Make 2)

With scrap white yarn, and dpn(s), CO 9 st. Join to work in the round.
Knit 2 rnds.
Inc Rnd: *K1f&b; rep from * to end of rnd—18 sts.
Knit 4 rnds.
Dec Rnd: *K2tog; rep from * to end of rnd—9 sts.
Knit 2 rnds.
Bind off all sts.
Carefully stuff with waste yarn and sew top closed. With black scrap yarn or embroidery thread, stitch eyes on, using photos as a guide. Sew the bottom of the eyes to the top of the hood using photos as a guide.

FINISHING

Sew buttons carefully on button band on opposite side matching buttonholes.
Carefully sew buttons opposite buttonholes along bum flap.
Weave in all ends. Wash and block to measurements.

Puppy

Babies and puppies are always a winning combination, aren't they? They can be the best of friends (unless they're fighting over the same person's attention, which always seems to be the case, doesn't it?). This puppy might wake you up just as many times a night as its real counterpart, but it sure is cute! You can have lots of fun with this one and really personalize it if you wish. Just use some of the techniques from Chapter 1 and you can change it up so you can have a matching pair of dogs in your house if you like.

Sizes: Newborn (6 months, 12 months, 18 months)

Finished Chest Circumference: 16 (18, 19, 20) in / 40.5 (45.5, 48.5, 51) cm

Gauge: 20 sts and 28 rows = 4 / 10 cm in St st on larger needles

Yarn: Space Cadet, Lyra (#3 light weight; 100% superwash merino wool; 270 yd / 245 m per 3.5 oz / 100 g): 2 (2, 3, 3) skeins Honey (MC) and 1 (1, 1, 1) skein Fat Free Chocolate (CC)

Needles: US 5 (3.75 mm), 16 in / 40 cm circular, or size needed to obtain gauge; US 4 (3.5 mm) 16 in / 40 cm circular and dpn(s), or needles one size smaller than size needed to obtain gauge

Notions: Tapestry needle, three ½ in / 1.5 cm JHB buttons, 1 in / 2.5 cm wide snap tape, sewing machine or sewing needle and thread, waste yarn

Stitch Guide

K1, P1 RIB WORKED FLAT

Row 1: *K1, p1; rep from * to end of row.
Row 2: *P1, k1; rep from * to end of row.
Repeat Rows 1 and 2 for pattern.

K1, P1 RIB IN THE ROUND

Rnd 1: *K1, p1; rep from * to end of rnd.
Repeat Rnd 1 for pattern.

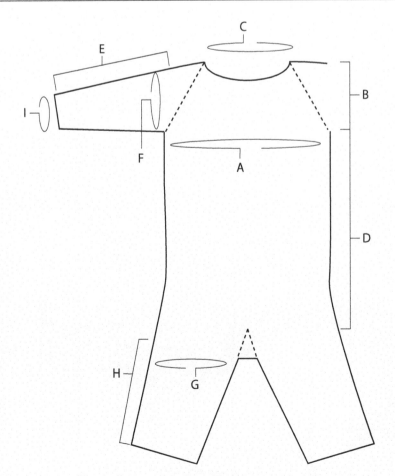

A - 16 (18, 19, 20) in
    40.5 (45.5, 48.5, 51) cm
B - 3.25 (3.75, 4, 4.25) in
    8.5 (9.5, 10, 11) cm
C - 9.5 (10.25, 10.75, 11.5) in
    24 (26, 27.5, 29) cm
D - 10.5 (13.5, 14.5, 15.5) in
    26.5 (34.5, 37, 39.5) cm
E - 7.5 (8.25, 9, 10) in
    19 (21, 23, 25.5) cm
F - 6.25 (7.25, 7.75, 8.5) in
    16 (18.5, 19.5, 21.5) cm
G - 8.25 (9, 9.5, 9.75) in
    21 (23, 24, 25) cm
H - 5.5 (6.5, 7.5, 8.5) in
    14 (16.5, 19, 21.5) cm
I - 5 (6, 6.5, 7.25) in
    12.5 (15, 16.5, 18.5) cm

INSTRUCTIONS

Body

With MC and larger needles, CO 47 (51, 54, 57) sts.

Set-up Row 1 (RS): K5 sts (button band), pm, k6 front sts, pm, k5 (6, 7, 8) sleeve sts, pm, 15 (17, 18, 19) back sts, pm, k5 (6, 7, 8) sleeve sts, pm, k6 front sts, pm, k5 sts (button band).

Set-up Row 2 (WS): K5, purl to last 5 sts, k5 (slipping all markers as you come to them).

Inc Row (RS): K5, sm, (knit to 1 st before m, k1f&b sm, k1f&b) 4 times, knit to end of row— 55 (59, 62, 65) sts.

Even Row (WS): K5, purl to last 5 sts, k5 (slipping all markers as you come to them).

Buttonhole Inc Row (RS): K2, yo, k2tog, k1, sm, (knit to 1 st before m, k1f&b sm, k1f&b) 4 times, knit to end of row—63 (67, 70, 73) sts.

Even Row (WS): K5, purl to last 5 sts, k5 (slipping all markers as you come to them).

Inc Row (RS): K5, sm, (knit to 1 st before m, k1f&b sm, k1f&b) 4 times, knit to end of row—8 sts increased.

Repeat last two rows 2 (3, 4, 4) times more—87 (99, 110, 113) sts.

Then work one more WS Even Row.

Buttonhole Inc Row (RS): K2, yo, k2tog, k1, sm, (knit to 1 st before m, k1f&b, sm, k1f&b) 4 times, knit to end of row—95 (107, 118, 121) sts.

Even Row (WS): K5, purl to last 5 sts, k5 (slipping all markers as you come to them).

Inc Row (RS): K5, sm, (knit to 1 st before m, k1f&b sm, k1f&b) 4 times, knit to end of row—8 sts increased.

Repeat last two rows 2 (3, 3, 4) times more—119 (139, 150, 161) sts.

Then work one more WS Even Row.

Buttonhole Inc Row (RS): K2, yo, k2tog, k1, sm, (knit to 1 st before m, k1f&b, sm, k1f&b) 4 times, knit to end of row—127 (147, 158, 169) sts.

Even Row (WS): K5, purl to last 5 sts, k5 (slipping all markers as you come to them).

Join Fronts and Back (RS): K5, sm, (knit to 1 st before m, k1f&b sm, k1f&b) 4 times, knit to last 5 sts. Slip 5 sts purlwise from the LH needle to spare dpn, then k2tog using 1 st from the RH needle and 1 st from dpn five times—130 (150, 161, 172) sts.

Separate Sleeves: Remove m, knit to next m, then move 27 (32, 35, 38) sleeve sts to waste yarn, CO 1 st, place new BOR m, CO 1 st,

FRONT

BACK

remove m, knit to next m, remove m, move 27
(32, 35, 38) sleeve sts to waste yarn, CO 1 st,
pm, CO 1 st, knit to end of rnd.
Knit every rnd until piece measures 10.5
(13.5, 14.5, 15.5) in / 26.5 (34.5, 37, 39.5) cm
from underarm.

Gusset

Set-up Rnd 1: *K19 (22, 23, 25) sts, place gusset
m, k1, place gusset m, k40 (45, 48, 50) sts,
place gusset m, k1, place gusset m, knit to end.
Set-up Rnd 2: Knit.
Gusset Inc Rnd: Knit to gusset m, sm, *m1L, knit
to m, m1R, sm; rep from * once, knit to end.
Even Rnd: Knit.
Repeat last 2 rnds four times more, until there
are 11 sts between the gusset markers.
Split Legs: Knit to last gusset m, slip next 11
sts to waste yarn, turn and purl back to the
back gusset sts, slip next 11 sts to waste yarn.
Continue working left leg only in St st flat,
until leg measures
3 (4, 5, 6) in / 7.5 (10, 12.5, 15) cm from split.
Switch to CC and work in St st flat for 1
in / 2.5 cm.
*Note: If preferred here, you can place the right
leg sts on waste yarn or a holder, but you can
easily leave them on the other portion of the
circular needle while working the left leg flat.*
Switch to smaller needles and work in K1, P1 Rib
for 1½ in / 4 cm.
Gusset Snap Band: With smaller needles and RS
facing and starting at the bottom right corner
of the front above the Rib stitch, pick up and
knit 2 sts for every 3 sts along the leg, move
the 11 held gusset sts on to spare needles and
knit across, pick up and knit 2 sts for every
3 sts along the leg. Knit every row for 1.5 in /
4 cm. Bind off all sts. Repeat for back side.

Sleeves

Move 27 (32, 35, 38) sleeve sts to dpns.
Reattach yarn and knit around sleeve sts, pick
up and knit 2 sts, pm, pick up and knit 2
sts—31 (36, 39, 42) sts.
Knit 3 rnds.
Dec Rnd: K1, k2tog, knit to last 3 sts before m,
ssk, k1—29 (34, 37, 40) sts.
Knit 10 (10, 12, 14) rnds.
Dec Rnd: K1, k2tog, knit to last 3 sts before m,
ssk, k1—27 (32, 35, 38) sts.
Knit 10 (10, 12, 14) rnds.

Dec Rnd: K1, k2tog, knit to last 3 sts before m, ssk, k1—25 (30, 33, 36) sts.

Knit until sleeve measures 4.5 (5.25, 6, 7) in / 11.5 (13.5, 15, 18) cm from underarm.

Switch to CC and knit for 1 in / 2.5 cm.

Final Dec Rnd (Sizes Newborn & 12 Month Only): K1, k2tog, knit to end—24 (30, 32, 36) sts.

Switch to smaller needles and work in K1, P1 Rib for 2 in / 5 cm.

Hood

Begin at right front edge with larger needles and MC, pick up and knit 36 (40, 40, 44) sts.

Next Row (WS): Purl.

Inc Row 1 (RS): *K1, k1f&b; rep from * to end— 54 (60, 60, 66) sts.

Next Row: Purl.

Inc Row 2: K0 (0, 0, 2), *k2, k1f&b; rep from * to end of row—72 (80, 80, 88) sts.

Work in St st until hood measures 7 (7, 7.5, 8) in / 18 (18, 19, 20.5) cm.

Using Kitchener stitch graft hood closed.

HOOD EDGING

With smaller needles and CC and beginning at right front edge after the button band, pick up and knit 2 sts for every 3 sts around the front, the hood, and the left front.

Work in K1, P1 Rib for 3 rows. Bind off in Rib pattern.

Ears (make 2)

Using dpn(s) and CC, starting about 1½ in / 4 cm from the top seam and about 2½ in / 6.5 cm from the edge of the hood, pick up and knit 8 sts, then pick up and knit 8 sts directly below those 8 sts, pm and knit for 10 rnds.

Inc Rnd: *K1, k1f&b; rep from * to end of rnd—24 sts.

Knit 2 rnds.

Inc Rnd: *K2, k1f&b; rep from * to end of rnd—32 sts.

Knit for 18 rnds.

Dec Rnd: *K2, k2tog; rep from * to end of rnd—24 sts.

Knit 1 rnd.

Dec Rnd: *K1, k2tog; rep from * to end of rnd—16 sts.

Dec Rnd: *K2tog; rep from * to end of rnd—8 sts.

Cut yarn and pull tight through remaining sts. Close hole, weave in yarn, and cut.

Repeat ear on other side.

FINISHING

Using a sewing machine, or needle and thread, sew snap tape on the gusset button band. Sew buttons opposite buttonholes. Weave in all ends. Wash and block.

Fox

What does the fox say? Think of all the fun playtimes you'll have with your little one in this sneaky but adorable outfit!

Sizes: Newborn (6 months, 12 months, 18 months)

Finished Chest Circumference: 16 (18, 20, 22) in / 40.5 (45.5, 51, 56) cm

Finished Head Circumference: 10.5 (12, 13.25, 14.5) in / 26.5 (30.5, 33.5, 37) cm

Gauge: 24 sts and 32 rows = 4 in / 10 cm in St st on larger needles

Yarn: Lorna's Laces, Shepherd Sport (#2 fine weight; 100% superwash merino wool; 200 yd / 183 m per 2 oz / 57 g); 1 (2, 2, 3) skeins Brick (MC), 1 skein Tan (CC)

Needles: US 5 (3.5 mm), 16 in / 40 cm circular, or size needed to obtain gauge; US 3 (3.75 mm) 16 in / 40 cm circular and dpn(s), or needles two sizes smaller than size needed to obtain gauge

Notions: Tapestry needle, 1 in / 2.5 cm wide snap tape, sewing needle and thread, waste yarn

Stitch Guide

K1, P1 RIB WORKED FLAT

Row 1: *K1, p1; rep from * to end of row.
Row 2: *P1, k1; rep from * to end of row.
Repeat Rows 1 and 2 for pattern.

K1, P1 RIB IN THE ROUND

Rnd 1: *K1, p1; rep from * to end of rnd.
Repeat Rnd 1 for pattern.

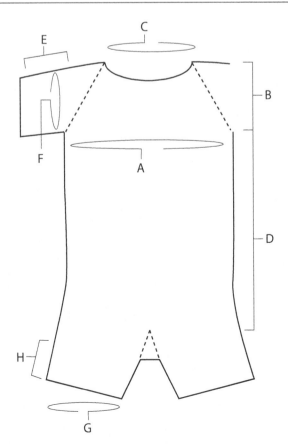

A - 16 (18, 20, 22) in
   40.5 (45.5, 51, 56) cm
B - 3.25 (3.5, 4, 4.25) in
   8.5 (9, 10, 11) cm
C - 9.5 (11, 11.75, 13.5) in
   24 (28, 30, 34.5) cm
D - 10.5 (13.5, 14.5, 15.5) in
   26.5 (34.5, 37, 39.5) cm
E - 2.5 in / 5 cm
F - 6 (6.5, 7.5, 8.25) in
   15 (16.5, 19, 21) cm
G - 9.5 (10.5, 11.5, 12.5) in
   24 (26.5, 29, 32) cm
H - 3 (3.5, 3.75, 4) in
   7.5 (9, 9.5, 10) cm

INSTRUCTIONS

Body

With CC and smaller needles, CO 47 (51, 57, 63) sts.

Set-up Row 1 (RS): K11 (11, 13, 13) front sts, pm, k6 (6, 6, 8) sleeve sts, pm, k16 (20, 22, 24) back sts, pm, k6 (6, 6, 8) sleeve sts, pm, k8 (8, 10, 10) front sts.

Set-up Row 2 (WS): Knit.

Set-up Row 3: Knit.

Buttonhole Row (WS): Knit to last 3 sts, k2tog, yo, k1.

Switch to larger needles and MC.

Inc Row (RS): (Knit to 1 st before m, k1f&b, sm, k1f&b) 4 times, knit to end—55 (59, 65, 71) sts.

Even Row (WS): K3, purl to last 3 sts, k3 (slipping all markers as you come to them).

Next Inc Row (RS): (Knit to 1 st before m, k1f&b, sm, k1f&b) 4 times, knit to end—63 (67, 73, 79) sts.

Buttonhole Row (WS): K3, purl to last 3 sts, k2tog, yo, k1.

Next Inc Row (RS): (Knit to 1 st before m, k1f&b, sm, k1f&b) 4 times, knit to end—71 (75, 81, 87) sts.

Row 8: K3, purl to last 3 sts, k3.

Joining Rnd (RS): Slip 3 sts purlwise from the RH needle to spare dpn, then k2tog using 1 st from RH needle and 1 st from dpn three times. Join to work in the round and place a different type of marker to distinguish the start of the round, (knit to 1 st before m, k1f&b, sm, k1f&b) 4 times, knit to end of rnd—76 (80, 86, 92) sts.

Even Rnd: Knit.

Inc Rnd: (Knit to 1 st before m, k1f&b, sm, k1f&b) 4 times, knit to end—84 (88, 94, 100) sts.

Repeat last 2 rnds 10 (12, 12, 13) times—164 (184, 190, 204) sts.

Separate Sleeves: Knit to 1st m, remove m, slip 36 (40, 40, 44) sleeve sts to waste yarn, CO 2 sts, remove m, knit to next marker, remove m, slip 36 (40, 40, 44) sleeve sts to waste yarn, CO 2 sts, remove m, knit to end of rnd—96 (108, 114, 120) sts.

Knit even until piece measures 10.5 (13.5, 14.5, 15.5) in / 26.5 (34.5, 37, 39.5) cm from underarm.

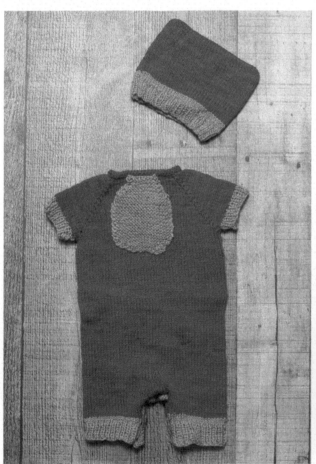

FRONT

BACK

Gusset

Set-up Rnd: K1, place gusset marker, k46 (52, 55, 58), place gusset marker, k2, place gusset marker, knit to 1 st before BOR, place gusset marker, k1.

Inc Rnd: Knit to gusset m, m1L, sm, knit to next gusset m, sm, m1R, knit to next gusset m, M1L, sm, knit to next gusset m, sm, M1R, knit to end. Repeat last 2 rnds until there are 11 sts between each set of gusset markers.

Split Legs: Knit to last gm, slip next 11 sts to waste yarn, turn and purl back to the back gusset sts, slip next 11 sts to waste yarn. Continue working left leg only in St st flat, until leg measures 2 (2.5, 2.75, 3) in / 5 (6.5, 7, 7.5) cm from split.

Note: If preferred here, you can place the right leg sts on waste yarn or a holder, but you can easily leave them on the other portion of the circular needle while working the left leg flat.

Change to smaller needles and CC, and work K1, P1 Rib for 1 in / 2.5 cm. Bind off in Rib pattern. Repeat for second leg.

Gusset Snap Band: With smaller needles and CC and the RS of the romper front facing, start at the bottom right corner, and pick up and knit 2 sts for every 3 rows along the leg, move the 11 held sts onto spare needles and knit across, pick up and knit 2 sts for every 3 rows down left side. Knit every row for 1.5 in / 4 cm. Bind off in Rib pattern. Repeat for back side.

Sleeves

Move 36 (40, 40, 44) sleeve sts to dpn(s). Knit around sleeve sts, pick up and knit 2 sts, pm, pick up and knit 2 sts. Knit 3 rnds.

Dec Rnd: K1, k2tog, knit to last 3 sts before m, ssk, k1—2 sts decreased.

Even Rnd: Knit.

Rep Dec Rnd 1 (1, 0, 1) time more—36 (40, 42, 44) sts.

Switch to smaller needles and CC and work in K1, P1 Rib in the round for 3 rnds. Bind off in Rib pattern.

NECK EDGING

With smaller needles, starting at the back of the neck, pick up and knit 2 sts for every 3 sts around neck edge. Bind off all sts purlwise.

Patch

With CC, CO 9 sts.

Knit 2 rows.

Inc Row: K1, k1f&b, knit to last 2 sts, k1f&b, k1—2 sts increased.

Next Row: Knit.

Rep these last 2 rows 4 more times—19 sts.

Knit 20 rows.

Dec Row: K1, ssk, knit to last 3 sts, k2tog, k1—2 sts decreased.

Next Row: Knit.

Rep these last 2 rows 4 more times—9 sts.

Bind off all sts knitwise.

Sew front patch to the front of romper, using photos as a guide.

FINISHING

Sew buttons carefully on button band on opposite side matching buttonholes.

Using a sewing machine, or needle and thread, carefully sew snap tape along the RS of the gusset snap band.

Weave in all ends. Wash and block to measurements.

Hat

With CC, CO 64 (72, 80, 84) sts, place marker and join to work in the round, being careful not to twist your stitches.

Rnd 1: *K2, p2; rep from * to end of round.

Repeat Rnd 1 until piece measures 1 in / 2.5 cm from cast-on edge.

Knit 4 rnds.

Switch to MC and continue to work in St st until hat measures 5.5 (6, 6.5, 7) in / 14 (15, 16.5, 18) cm from CO edge.

Flip piece inside out. Hold circular needles so that LH and RH needles are parallel and are both held in LH. Insert DPN as if to knit into the first st on both needles simultaneously and knit one stitch. Slip both sts off circular needle, one st is now on DPN. Repeat for second st, then pass first stitch on DPN over second stitch in normal cast-off procedure. Repeat process until all sts are bound off. Cut yarn, weave through last st, and pull tight to secure.

Cat

There are cat people and there are dog people (for the record, I am definitely a cat person, but our dog, Bear, is slowly converting me to a sometimes dog person!). My very favorite type of cat, though, is the barn cat! This colorway from The Fiber Seed just reminds me so much of that quintessential and oh-so-special feline. The headband with cat ears makes this piece really shine, so make sure you don't forget to make one (I kind of want to make one in my size!).

Romper Sizes: Newborn (6 months, 12 months, 18 months)

Headband Sizes: Newborn to 12 months (18 months)

Finished Chest Circumference: 16 (18, 20, 22) in / 40.5(45.5, 51, 56) cm

Gauge: 20 sts/28 rows = 4 in / 10 cm in St st on larger needles

Yarn: The Fiber Seed, Sprout Worsted (#4 medium weight; 90% superwash merino wool, 10% nylon; 250 yd / 230 m per 4.8 oz / 136 g): 2 (2, 3, 3) skeins Sunset Silhouette

Needles: US 7 (4.5 mm) 16 in / 40 cm circular, or size needed to obtain gauge; US 5 (3.75 mm) 16 in / 40 cm circular and dpn(s), or needles two sizes smaller than size needed to obtain gauge

Notions: Tapestry needle, three ½ in / 1.5 cm JHB buttons, 1 in / 2.5 cm wide snap tape, sewing thread, waste yarn

Stitch Guide

K1, P1 RIB WORKED FLAT

Row 1: *K1, p1; rep from * to end of row.
Row 2: *P1, k1; rep from * to end of row.
Repeat Rows 1 and 2 for pattern.

K1, P1 RIB IN THE ROUND

Rnd 1: *K1, p1; rep from * to end of rnd.
Repeat Rnd 1 for pattern.

INSTRUCTIONS

Body

With larger needles, CO 49 (51, 55, 59) sts.

Set-up Row 1 (RS): K5 sts (button band), pm, k6 (6, 7, 7) front sts, pm, k6 (6, 7, 8) sleeve sts, pm, k15 (17, 17, 19) back sts, pm, k6 (6, 7, 8) sleeve sts, pm, k6 (6, 7, 7) front sts, pm, k5 sts (button band).

Set-up Row 2 (WS): K5, purl to last 5 sts, k5 (slipping all markers as you come to them).

Inc Row (RS): K5, sm, (knit to 1 st before m, k1f&b sm, k1f&b) 4 times, knit to end of row—57 (59, 63, 67) sts.

Even Row (WS): K5, purl to last 5 sts, k5 (slipping all markers as you come to them).

Buttonhole Inc Row (RS): K2, yo, k2tog, k1, sm, (knit to 1st before m, k1f&b, sm, k1f&b) 4 times, knit to end of row—65 (67, 71, 75) sts.

Even Row (WS): K5, purl to last 5 sts, k5 (slipping all markers as you come to them).

Inc Row (RS): K5, sm, (knit to 1 st before m, k1f&b sm, k1f&b) 4 times, knit to end of row—8 sts increased.

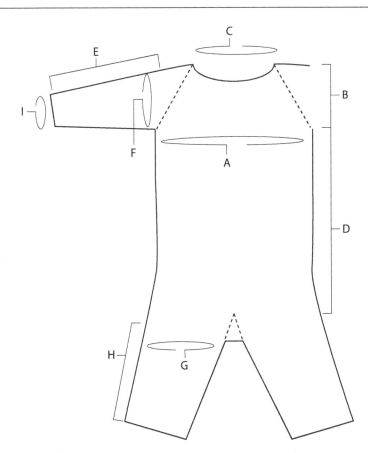

A - 16 (18, 20, 22) in
 40.5 (45.5, 51, 56) cm
B - 2.75 (3.5, 4, 4.5) in
 7 (9, 10, 11.5) cm
C - 9.75 (10.25, 11, 11.75) in
 25 (26, 28, 30) cm
D - 10.5 (13.5, 14.5, 15.5) in
 26.5 (34.5, 37, 39.5) cm
E - 7.5 (8.25, 9, 10) in
 19 (21, 23, 25.5) cm
F - 6 (6.75, 7.75, 8.75) in
 15 (17, 19.5, 22) cm
G - 8.25 (9, 9.75, 10.75) in
 21 (23, 25, 27.5) cm
H - 5.5 (6.5, 7.5, 8.5) in
 14 (16.5, 19, 21.5) cm
I - 4.75 (5.5, 6.5, 7.5) in
 12 (14, 16.5, 19) cm

Repeat last two rows 2 (3, 4, 5) times more—89 (99, 111, 123) sts.

Then work one more WS Even Row.

Buttonhole Inc Row (RS): K2, yo, k2tog, k1, sm, (knit to 1st before m, k1f&b, sm, k1f&b) 4 times, knit to end of row—97 (107, 119, 131) sts.

Even Row (WS): K5, purl to last 5 sts, k5 (slipping all markers as you come to them).

Inc Row (RS): K5, sm, (knit to 1 st before m, k1f&b sm, k1f&b) 4 times, knit to end of row—8 sts increased.

Repeat last two rows 1 (2, 3, 4) times more—113 (131, 151, 171) sts.

Then work one more WS Even Row.

Buttonhole Inc Row (RS): K2, yo, k2tog, k1, sm, (knit to 1st before m, k1f&b, sm, k1f&b) 4 times, knit to end of row—121 (139, 159, 179) sts.

Even Row (WS): K5, purl to last 5 sts, k5 (slipping all markers as you come to them).

Joining Row (RS): K5, sm, (knit to 1 st before m, k1f&b sm, k1f&b) 4 times, knit to last 5 sts. Slip 5 sts purlwise from the LH needle to spare dpn, then k2tog using 1 st from the RH needle and 1 st from dpn five times—124 (142, 162, 182) sts.

Cut yarn, leaving a 12 in / 30.5 cm tail, slip 16 (18, 21, 23) sts purlwise to RH needle (all the sts before the first sleeve m).

Separate Sleeves: Remove m, then move 26 (30, 35, 40) sleeve sts to waste yarn, CO 2 sts, place new BOR m, CO 2 sts, remove m, knit to next m, remove m, move 26 (30, 35, 40) sleeve sts to waste yarn, CO 2 sts, pm, CO 2 sts, knit to end of rnd. Knit every rnd until piece measures 10.5 (13.5, 14.5, 15.5) in / 26.5 (34.5, 37, 39.5) cm from underarm.

Gusset

Set-up Rnd 1: *K19 (22, 24, 27) sts, place gusset m, k1, place gusset m, k39 (44, 49, 54) sts, place gusset m, k1, place gusset m, knit to end.

Set-up Rnd 2: Knit.

Gusset Inc Rnd: Knit to gusset m, sm, *m1L, knit to m, m1R, sm; rep from * once, knit to end.

Even Rnd: Knit.

Repeat last 2 rnds four times more, until there are 11 sts between the gusset markers.

Split Legs: Knit to last gusset m, slip next 11 sts to waste yarn, turn and purl back to the back gusset sts, slip next 11 sts to waste yarn. Continue working left leg only in St st flat,

FRONT

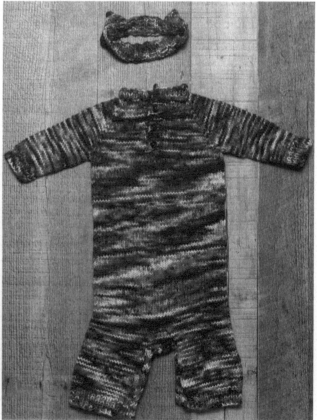

BACK

until leg measures 4 (5, 6, 7) in / 10 (12.5, 15, 18) cm from split.

Note: If preferred here, you can place the right leg sts on waste yarn or a holder, but you can easily leave them on the other portion of the circular needle while working the left leg flat.

Switch to smaller needles and work in K1, P1 Rib for 1.5 in / 4 cm.

Gusset Snap Band: With smaller needles and RS facing and starting at the bottom right corner of the front above the Rib stitch, pick up and knit 2 sts for every 3 sts along the leg, move the 11 held gusset sts on to spare needles and knit across, pick up and knit 2 sts for every 3 sts along the leg. Knit every row for 1.5 in / 4 cm. Bind off all sts. Repeat for back side.

Sleeves

Move 26 (30, 35, 40) sleeve sts to dpns.

Reattach yarn and knit around sleeve sts, pick up and knit 2 sts, pm, pick up and knit 2 sts—30 (34, 39, 44) sts.

Knit 3 rnds.

Dec Rnd: K1, k2tog, knit to last 3 sts before m, ssk, k1—28 (32, 37, 42) sts.

Knit 10 (10, 12, 14) rnds.

Dec Rnd: K1, k2tog, knit to last 3 sts before m, ssk, k1—26 (30, 35, 40) sts.

Knit 10 (10, 12, 14) rnds.

Dec Rnd: K1, k2tog, knit to last 3 sts before m, ssk, k1—24 (28, 33, 38) sts.

Knit until sleeve measures 5.5 (6.25, 7, 8, 9) in / 14 (16, 18, 20.5, 23) cm from underarm.

Final Dec Rnd (Size 12 Month Only): K1, k2tog, knit to end—24 (28, 32, 38) sts.

Switch to smaller needles and work in K1, P1 Rib for 2 in / 5 cm. Bind off all sts in Rib pattern.

NECK EDGING

With smaller needles, starting at the back of the neck, pick up and knit 2 sts for every 3 sts around neck edge.

Work in K1, P1 Rib for 3 rows. Bind off all sts in Rib pattern.

FINISHING

Sew buttons carefully on button band on opposite side matching buttonholes.

Using a sewing machine, or needle and thread, carefully sew snap tape along the RS of the gusset snap band.

Weave in all ends. Wash and block to measurements.

Headband

CO 68 (76) sts, pm, and join to work in the rnd.

Rnds 1–8: *K3, p1; rep from * to end of rnd.

Bind off all sts in pattern.

Ears (make 2)

Using dpn(s), CO 20 sts, pm, and join to work in the rnd.

Rnds 1 and 2: Knit.

Rnd 3: *Ssk, k6, k2tog; rep from * once—16 sts.

Rnd 4: Knit.

Rnd 5: *Ssk, k4, k2tog; rep from * once—12 sts.

Rnd 6: Knit.

Rnd 7: *Ssk, k2, k2tog; rep from * once—8 sts.

Rnd 8: Knit.

Rnd 9: *Ssk, k2tog; rep from * once—4 sts.

Rnd 10: *K2tog; rep from * once—2 sts.

Cut yarn and pull tight through remaining 2 sts.

Sew ears to top of headband, using photos as a guide.

Because your little friend wants to be a cat, too!

Size: To fit a 15 in / 38 cm Waldorf-style doll

Gauge: 20 sts and 28 rows = 4 in / 10 cm in St st

Yarn: The Fiber Seed, Sprout Worsted (#4 medium weight; 90% superwash merino wool, 10% nylon; 250 yd / 230 m per 4.8 oz / 136 g): 1 skein Sunset Silhouette

Needles: US 7 (4.5 mm) 16 in / 40 cm circular and dpn(s)

Notions: Snap tape, measuring tape, tapestry needle, sewing needle and thread

Stitch Guide

K1, P1 RIB IN THE ROUND

Rnd 1: *K1, p1; rep from * to end of rnd.
Repeat Rnd 1 for pattern.

INSTRUCTIONS

Body

With circular needles, CO 46 sts as follows: CO 4 (snap band), pm, CO 6 (back), pm, CO 5 (sleeve), pm, CO 16 (front), pm, CO 5 (sleeve), pm, CO 6 (back), pm, CO 4 (snap band).

Set-up Row 1 (RS): K4, work in k1, p1 rib to last 4 sts, k4.

Set-up Row 2 (WS): K4, work in k1, p1 rib to last 4 sts, k4.

Inc Row (RS): K4, sm, (knit to 1 st before m, k1f&b sm, k1f&b) 4 times, knit to end of row—54 sts.

Even Row (WS): K4, purl to last 4 sts, k4 (slipping all markers as you come to them).
Repeat last two rows 13 times more—126 sts.
Then work one more WS Even Row.

Joining Row (RS): K4, sm, (knit to 1 st before m, k1f&b sm, k1f&b) 4 times, knit to last 4 sts. Slip 4 sts purlwise from the LH needle to spare dpn, then k2tog using 1 st from the RH needle and 1 st from dpn four times—130 sts.

Separate Sleeves: Knit to next m, remove m, then move 27 sleeve sts to waste yarn, remove m, CO 1 st, place new BOR m, CO 1 st, knit to next m, remove m, move 37 sleeve sts to waste yarn, CO 2 sts, knit to end of rnd.
Knit every rnd until piece measures 5.5 in / 14 cm from underarm.

Gusset

Set-up Rnd 1: K20, place gusset m, M1R, place gusset m, k40, place gusset m, M1R, place gusset m, knit to end.

Set-up Rnd 2: Knit.

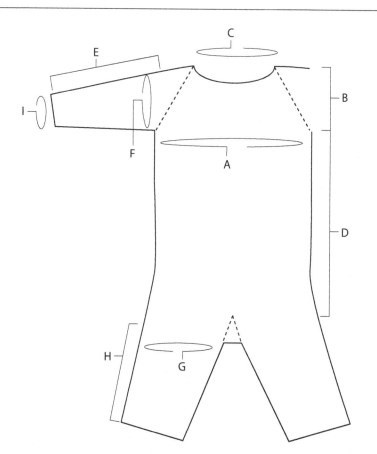

A - 16 in [40.5 cm]

B - 3.75 in [9.5 cm]

C - 9 in [23 cm]

D - 5.5 in [14 cm]

E - 2 in [5 cm]

F - 6 in [15 cm]

G - 8 in [20.5 cm]

H - 3.75 in [9.5 cm]

I - 5.25 in [13.5 cm]

Gusset Inc Rnd: (Knit to gusset m, sm, M1L, knit to gusset m, m1R, sm) twice, knit to end.
Even Rnd: Knit.
Repeat last 2 rnds twice more, until there are 7 sts between the gusset markers.
Split Legs: Knit to gusset m, move 7 gusset sts to waste yarn, move leg sts to another piece of waste yarn. Then move second set of 7 gusset sts to another piece of waste yarn. Using dpns, knit the first set of leg sts in the round.
Work in the round until leg measures 3 in / 7.5 cm from split.
Work in K1, P1 Rib for 4 rnds. Bind off all sts in Rib pattern.
Place sts from second leg on dpns and work as first.
Place gusset sts on separate dpns and use the kitchener stitch to graft the gusset sts together.

Sleeves

Move 27 sleeve sts to dpns.
Reattach yarn and knit around sleeve sts, pick up and knit 1 st, pm, pick up and knit 1 st—29 sts.
Knit 2 rnds.
Dec Rnd: K1, k2tog, knit to last 3 sts before m, ssk, k1—27 sts.
Even Rnd: Knit.

Repeat last two rnds once more—25 sts.
Final Dec Rnd: K1, k2tog, knit to end—24 sts.
Work in K1, P1 Rib for 4 rnds. Bind off all sts in Rib pattern.

FINISHING

Weave in all ends.
Sew snap tape on back neck band.
Wash and block to measurements.

Headband

CO 52 sts, pm, and join to work in the rnd.
Rnd 1: *K3, p1; rep from * to end of rnd.
Repeat Rnd 1 for 7 more rnds.
Bind off all sts in pattern.

Ears (make 2)

Using dpn(s), CO 12 sts, pm, and join to work in the rnd.
Rnds 1 and 2: Knit.
Rnd 3: *Ssk, k2, k2tog; rep from * once—8 sts.
Rnds 4 and 5: Knit.
Rnd 6: *Ssk, k2tog; rep from * once—4 sts.
Rnd 7: Knit.
Rnd 8: *K2tog; rep from * once—2 sts.
Cut yarn and pull tight through remaining 2 sts.
Sew ears to top of headband, using photos as a guide.

Giraffe

When we lived in Arizona, one of the highlights of our trips to the zoo was getting to feed the giraffes. Such beautiful, graceful, and majestic animals. They have a pattern unique to them, and in this romper, you have a chance to create something very special yourself. You aren't limited in the number of spots you make for your giraffe or where you place them, and you don't have to stick with traditional giraffe colors either. Let your imagination soar and make it your own.

Sizes: Newborn (6 months, 12 months, 18 months)

Finished Chest Circumference: 16 (18, 19, 20) in / 40.5 (45.5, 48.5, 51) cm

Gauge: 20 sts and 28 rows = 4 in / 10 cm in St st on larger needles

Yarn: Tippy Tree Yarns, Super DK (#3 light weight; 100% superwash merino; 231 yd / 211 m per 3.5 oz / 100 g): 1 (1, 2, 2) skeins Autumn Sunset Sky (MC) and 1 (1, 1, 1) skein Pinecone (CC)

Needles: US 5 (3.75 mm) 16 in / 40 cm circular, or size needed to obtain gauge; US 4 (3.5 mm) 16 in / 40 cm circular and dpn(s), or needles one size smaller than size needed to obtain gauge

Notions: Tapestry needle, three ½ in / 1.5 cm JHB buttons, 1 in / 2.5 cm wide snap tape, sewing machine or sewing needle and thread, waste yarn

Stitch Guide

K1, P1 RIB WORKED FLAT

Row 1: *K1, p1; rep from * to end of row.
Row 2: *P1, k1; rep from * to end of row.
Repeat Rows 1 and 2 for pattern.

K1, P1 RIB IN THE ROUND

Rnd 1: *K1, p1; rep from * to end of rnd.
Repeat Rnd 1 for pattern.

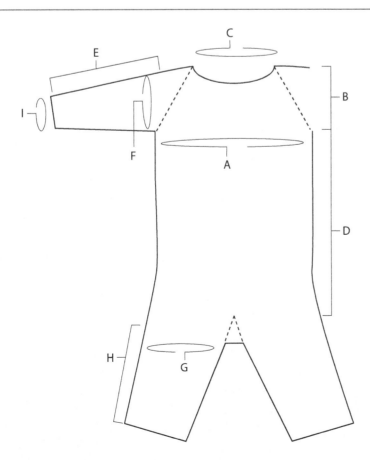

A - 16 (18, 19, 20) in
40.5 (45.5, 48.5, 51) cm
B - 3.25 (3.75, 4, 4.25) in
8.5 (9.5, 10, 11) cm
C - 9.5 (10.25, 10.75, 11.5) in
24 (26, 27.5, 29) cm
D - 10.5 (13.5, 14.5, 15.5) in
26.5 (34.5, 37, 39.5) cm
E - 7.5 (8.25, 9, 10) in
19 (21, 23, 25.5) cm
F - 6.25 (7.25, 7.75, 8.5) in
16 (18.5, 19.5, 21.5) cm
G - 8.25 (9, 9.5, 9.75) in
21 (23, 24, 25) cm
H - 4.5 (4.5, 5.5, 5.5) in
11.5 (11.5, 14, 14) cm
I - 5 (6, 6.5, 7.25) in
12.5 (15, 16.5, 18.5) cm

INSTRUCTIONS

Body

With larger needles and MC, CO 47 (51, 54, 57) sts.

Set-up Row 1 (RS): K5 sts (button band), pm, k6 front sts, pm, k5 (6, 7, 8) sleeve sts, pm, 15 (17, 18, 19) back sts, pm, k5 (6, 7, 8) sleeve sts, pm, k6 front sts, pm, k5 sts (button band).

Set-up Row 2 (WS): K5, purl to last 5 sts, k5 (slipping all markers as you come to them).

Inc Row (RS): K5, sm, (knit to 1 st before m, k1f&b sm, k1f&b) 4 times, knit to end of row—55 (59, 62, 65) sts.

Even Row (WS): K5, purl to last 5 sts, k5 (slipping all markers as you come to them).

Buttonhole Inc Row (RS): K2, yo, k2tog, k1, sm, (knit to 1st before m, k1f&b, sm, k1f&b) 4 times, knit to end of row—63 (67, 70, 73) sts.

Even Row (WS): K5, purl to last 5 sts, k5 (slipping all markers as you come to them).

Inc Row (RS): K5, sm, (knit to 1 st before m, k1f&b sm, k1f&b) 4 times, knit to end of row—8 sts increased.

Repeat last two rows 2 (3, 4, 4) times more—87 (99, 110, 113) sts.

Then work one more WS Even Row.

Buttonhole Inc Row (RS): K2, yo, k2tog, k1, sm, (knit to 1st before m, k1f&b, sm, k1f&b) 4 times, knit to end of row—95 (107, 118, 121) sts.

Even Row (WS): K5, purl to last 5 sts, k5 (slipping all markers as you come to them).

Inc Row (RS): K5, sm, (knit to 1 st before m, k1f&b sm, k1f&b) 4 times, knit to end of row—8 sts increased.

Repeat last two rows 2 (3, 3, 4) times more—119 (139, 150, 161) sts.

Then work one more WS Even Row.

Buttonhole Inc Row (RS): K2, yo, k2tog, k1, sm, (knit to 1st before m, k1f&b, sm, k1f&b) 4 times, knit to end of row—127 (147, 158, 169) sts.

Even Row (WS): K5, purl to last 5 sts, k5 (slipping all markers as you come to them).

Joining Row (RS): K5, sm, (knit to 1 st before m, k1f&b sm, k1f&b) 4 times, knit to last 5 sts. Slip 5 sts purlwise from the LH needle to spare dpn, then k2tog using 1 st from the RH needle and 1 st from dpn five times—130 (150, 161, 172) sts.

Separate Sleeves: Remove m, knit to next m, then move 27 (32, 35, 38) sleeve sts to waste yarn, CO 1 st, place new BOR m, CO 1 st, remove m, knit to next m, remove m, move 27 (32, 35, 38) sleeve sts to waste yarn, CO 1 st, pm, CO 1 st, knit to end of rnd.

FRONT

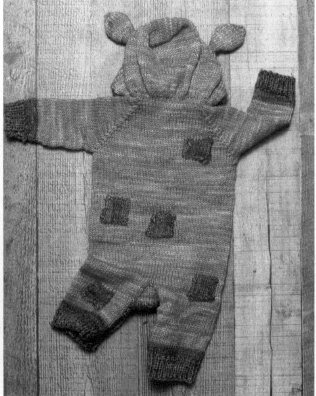

BACK

Knit every rnd until piece measures 10.5 (13.5, 14.5, 15.5) in / 26.5 (34.5, 37, 39.5) cm from underarm.

Gusset

Set-up Rnd 1: *K19 (22, 23, 25) sts, place gusset m, k1, place gusset m, k40 (45, 48, 50) sts, place gusset m, k1, place gusset m, knit to end.

Set-up Rnd 2: Knit.

Gusset Inc Rnd: Knit to gusset m, sm, *m1L, knit to m, m1R, sm; rep from * once, knit to end.

Even Rnd: Knit.

Repeat last 2 rnds four times more, until there are 11 sts between the gusset markers.

Split Legs: Knit to last gusset m, slip next 11 sts to waste yarn, turn and purl back to the back gusset sts, slip next 11 sts to waste yarn. Continue working left leg only in St st flat, until leg measures 2 (2, 3, 3) in / 5 (5, 7.5, 7.5) cm from split. Switch to CC and work in St st flat for 1 in / 2.5 cm.

Note: If preferred here, you can place the right leg sts on waste yarn or a holder, but you can easily leave them on the other portion of the circular needle while working the left leg flat.

Switch to smaller needles and work in K1, P1 Rib for 1.5 in / 4 cm.

Gusset Snap Band: With smaller needles and RS facing and starting at the bottom right corner of the front above the Rib stitch, pick up and knit 2 sts for every 3 sts along the leg, move the 11 held gusset sts on to spare needles and knit across, pick up and knit 2 sts for every 3 sts along the leg. Knit every row for 1.5 in / 4 cm. Bind off all sts. Repeat for back side.

Back Gusset Band

With smaller needles and with RS facing, start at the bottom right pick up and knit 2 sts for every 3 sts along the leg, move the 11 held sts on to spare needles and knit across, pick up and knit 2 sts for every 3 sts along the leg, making sure to end with an even number of sts. Work in K1, P1 Rib for 7 Rows. Bind off all sts in Rib pattern.

Sleeves

Move 27 (32, 35, 38) sleeve sts to dpns.

Reattach yarn and knit around sleeve sts, pick up and knit 2 sts, pm, pick up and knit 2 sts—31 (36, 39, 42) sts.

Knit 3 rnds.

Dec Rnd: K1, k2tog, knit to last 3 sts before m, ssk, k1—29 (34, 37, 40) sts.

Knit 10 (10, 12, 14) rnds.

Dec Rnd: K1, k2tog, knit to last 3 sts before m, ssk, k1—27 (32, 35, 38) sts.

Knit 10 (10, 12, 14) rnds.

Dec Rnd: K1, k2tog, knit to last 3 sts before m, ssk, k1—25 (30, 33, 36) sts.

Knit until sleeve measures 4.5 (5.25, 6, 7, 8) in / 11.5 (13.5, 15, 17, 20.5) cm from underarm.

Final Dec Rnd (Sizes Newborn and 12 Month Only): K1, k2tog, knit to end—24 (30, 32, 36) sts.

Switch to CC and knit for 1 in / 2.5 cm.

Switch to smaller needles and work in K1, P1 Rib for 1 in / 2.5 cm.

Bind off all sts in Rib pattern.

Hood

Begin at right front edge with larger needles, pick up and knit 36 (40, 40, 44) sts.

Next Row (WS): Purl.

Inc Row 1 (RS): *K1, k1f&b; rep from * to end—54 (60, 60, 66) sts.

Next Row: Purl.

Inc Row 2: *K2, k1f&b; rep from * to end of row—72 (80, 80, 88) sts.

Work in St st until hood measures 7 (7, 7.5, 8) in / 18 (18, 19, 20.5) cm.

Using Kitchener stitch graft hood closed.

HOOD EDGING

With smaller needles and beginning at right front edge after the button band, pick up and knit 2 sts for every 3 sts around the fronts, the hood, and the left front.

Work in K1, P1 Rib for 3 rows. Bind off in Rib pattern.

Spots (make 10)

With CC, CO 10 sts.

Work in St st for 1.5 in / 4 cm. Bind off all sts knitwise, leaving a 12 in / 30.5 cm tail.

Sew spots to body where desired, using photos as a guide.

Ears (make 2)

OUTER EAR (MAKE 2)

Leaving a long tail, with MC, CO 10 sts.

Work in St st for 1 in / 2.5 cm.

Inc Row (RS): K1, m1L, knit to last st, m1R, k1—12 sts.

Next Row: Purl.

Inc Row (RS): Repeat Inc Row—14 sts.

Continue in St st until the ear measures 2 in / 5 cm from the CO edge.

Dec Row (RS): K1, ssk, knit to last 3 sts, k2tog, k1—12 sts.

Next Row: Purl.

Dec Row: K1, ssk, knit to last 3 sts, k2tog, k1—10 sts.

Dec Row: P1, p2tog, purl to last 3 sts, p2tog, p1—8 sts.

Dec Row: K1, ssk, k2, k2tog, k1—6 sts.

Dec Row: P1, (p2tog) twice, p1—4 sts.

Dec Row: Ssk, k2tog—2 sts.

Dec Row: P2tog—1 st.

Cut the yarn, leaving a 12 in / 30.5 cm tail, pull through the remaining st.

INNER EAR (MAKE 2)

With CC, CO 8 sts.

Work in St st until piece measures .75 in / 2 cm.

Inc Row: K1, m1L, knit to last st, m1R, k1—10 sts.

Next Row (WS): Purl.

Inc Row: K1, m1L, knit to last st, m1R, k1—12 sts.

Continue in St st until the piece measures 1.75 in / 4.5 cm from CO edge.

Dec Row (RS): K1, ssk, knit to last 3 sts, k2tog, k1—10 sts.

Next Row (WS): Purl.

Dec Row: K1, ssk, knit to last 3 sts, k2tog, k1—8 sts.

Dec Row: P1, p2tog, purl to last 3 sts, p2tog, p1—6 sts.

Dec Row: K1, ssk, k2tog, k1—4 sts.

Dec Row: (P2tog) twice—2 sts.

Dec Row: K2tog—1 st.

Cut the yarn and pull tight through the remaining st.

ASSEMBLY

Place the inner ear piece on top of the outer ear piece, with WS facing each other. Whipstich the inner ear and outer ear together along the edges. Sew the CO edges together, then carefully sew the ear to the side and top of the hood, using the photos as a guide.

FINISHING

Using a sewing machine, or needle and thread, sew snap tape on the gusset button band.

Sew buttons opposite buttonholes.

Weave in all ends. Wash and block.

Lion

"Roar!" says the lion. This piece is so snuggly, so warm, and just so very fun. Your little one will have so much fun pretending to be the King (or Queen!) of the jungle. The flap in the back makes for quick changes, too, so you are all set to keep playing all day.

Sizes: Newborn (6 months, 12 months, 18 months)

Finished Chest Circumference: 16 (18, 20, 22) in / 40.5 (45.5, 51, 56) cm

Gauge: 24 sts and 32 rows = 4 in / 10 cm in St st on larger needles

Yarn: Knit One Crochet Too, Sebago (#3 light weight; 100% Australia merino super wash wool; 146 yd / 133.5 m per 1.7 oz / 50 g): 2 (2, 3, 3) skeins #301 Honey (MC); 2 (2, 3, 3) skeins #462 Nutmeg (C1); and 1 (1, 1, 1) skein #843 Coffee (C2)

Needles: US 4 (3.5 mm) 16 in / 40 cm circulars and dpns, or size needed to obtain gauge; US 3 (3.25 mm) 16 in / 40 cm circular and dpns, or needles one size smaller than needed to obtain gauge

Notions: Tapestry needle, three 0.5 in / 1.5 cm JHB buttons, six 1 in / 2.5 cm buttons for back flap

Stitch Guide

K1, P1 RIB WORKED FLAT

Row 1: *K1, p1; rep from * to end of row.
Row 2: *P1, k1; rep from * to end of row.
Repeat Rows 1 and 2 for pattern.

K1, P1 RIB IN THE ROUND

Rnd 1: *K1, p1; rep from * to end of rnd.
Repeat Rnd 1 for pattern.

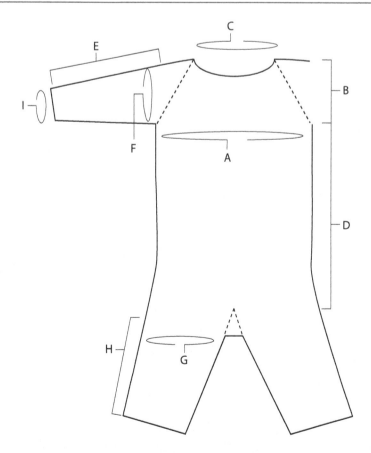

A - 16 (18, 20, 22) in
    40.5 (45.5, 51, 56) cm
B - 3.5 (3.5, 3.75, 4) in
    9 (9, 9.5, 10) cm
C - 7.75 (10, 11.75, 13) in
    19.5 (25.5, 30, 33) cm
D - 10.5 (13.5, 14.5, 15.5) in
    26.5 (34.5, 37, 39.5) cm
E - 5 (6, 8, 8) in
    15 (15, 20.5, 20.5) cm
F - 7.5 (7.75, 8.5, 8.75) in
    19 (19.5, 21.5, 22) cm
G - 5.75 (5.75, 6.25, 6.75) in
    14.5 (14.5, 16, 17) cm
H - 5 (6, 7, 8) in
    12.5 (15, 18, 20.5) cm
I - 5.25 (5.5, 6, 6.25) in
    13.5 (14, 15, 16) cm

INSTRUCTIONS

Body

With larger needles and C1, provisionally CO 46 (60, 70, 78) sts.

Set-up Row 1 (RS): K4 sts (button band), pm, k5 (9, 11, 13) front sts, pm, k6 (7, 8, 8) sleeve sts, pm, k16 (20, 24, 28) back sts, pm, k6 (7, 8, 8) sleeve sts, pm, k5 (9, 11, 13) front sts, pm, k4 sts (button band).

Set-up Row 2 (WS): K4, purl to last 4 sts, k4 (slipping all markers as you come to them).

Inc Row (RS): K4, sm, (knit to 1 st before m, k1f&b sm, k1f&b) 4 times, knit to end of row—54 (68, 78, 86) sts.

Even Row (WS): K4, purl to last 4 sts, k4 (slipping all markers as you come to them).

Buttonhole Inc Row (RS): K1, yo, k2tog, k1, sm, (knit to 1st before m, k1f&b, sm, k1f&b) 4 times, knit to end of row—62 (76, 86, 94) sts.

Even Row (WS): K4, purl to last 4 sts, k4 (slipping all markers as you come to them).

Inc Row (RS): K4, sm, (knit to 1 st before m, k1f&b sm, k1f&b) 4 times, knit to end of row—8 sts increased.

Repeat last two rows 3 (3, 4, 4) times more—94 (108, 126, 134) sts.

Then work one more WS Even Row.

Buttonhole Inc Row (RS): K1, yo, k2tog, k1, sm, (knit to 1st before m, k1f&b, sm, k1f&b) 4 times, knit to end of row—102 (116, 134, 142) sts.

Even Row (WS): K4, purl to last 4 sts, k4 (slipping all markers as you come to them).

Inc Row (RS): K4, sm, (knit to 1 st before m, k1f&b sm, k1f&b) 4 times, knit to end of row—8 sts increased.

Repeat last two rows 3 (3, 3, 4) times more—134 (148, 166, 182) sts.

Then work one more WS Even Row.

Buttonhole Inc Row (RS): K1, yo, k2tog, k1, sm, (knit to 1st before m, k1f&b, sm, k1f&b) 4 times, knit to end of row—142 (156, 174, 190) sts.

Even Row (WS): K4, purl to last 4 sts, k4 (slipping all markers as you come to them).

Inc Row (RS): K4, sm, (knit to 1 st before m, k1f&b sm, k1f&b) 4 times, knit to end of row—150 (164, 182, 198) sts.

Joining Row (RS): K4, sm, (knit to 1 st before m, k1f&b sm, k1f&b) 4 times, knit to last 4 sts. Slip 4 sts purlwise from the LH needle to

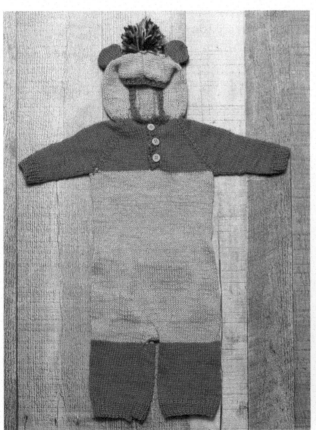

FRONT

BACK

spare dpn, then k2tog using 1 st from the RH needle and 1 st from dpn four times—154 (168, 186, 202) sts.

Cut yarn, leaving a 12 in / 30.5 cm tail, slip 19 (23, 26, 29) sts purlwise to the RH needle (all the sts before the first sleeve m).

Separate Sleeves: Remove m, then move 34 (35, 38, 40) sleeve sts to waste yarn, this next m becomes new BOR m, CO 5 sts, knit to next m, remove m, move 34 (35, 38, 40) sleeve sts to waste yarn, remove m, CO 5 sts, knit to end of rnd—96 (108, 120, 132) body sts.

Switch to MC and knit every rnd until piece measures 5 (6, 8, 8) in / 12.5 (15, 20.5, 20.5) cm.

Next Rnd: K17 (17, 19, 20) work in K2, P2 Rib for 20 (24, 26, 30) sts, continue to knit around.

Work in this manner for 1 in / 2.5 cm.

Then k17 (17, 19, 20), bind off 20 (24, 26, 30) sts in Rib pattern, knit to the end of the rnd.

Work flat in St st for 4 (4.5, 5, 6) in / 10 (11.5, 12.5, 15) cm, ending with a WS row.

On the next row, knit to the end of the row, and CO 20 (24, 26, 30) sts.

Knit 4 rnds.

Gusset

Set-up Rnd 1: K26 (28, 31, 34) sts, place gusset m, k2, place gusset m, k 46 (52, 58, 64) sts, place gusset m, k1, place gusset m, knit to end.

Set-up Rnd 2: Knit.

Gusset Inc Rnd: Knit to gusset m, sm, *m1L, knit to m, m1R, sm; rep from * once, knit to end.

Even Rnd: Knit.

Repeat last 2 rnds four times more, until there are 12 sts between the gusset markers.

Split Legs: Knit to gusset m, move 12 gusset sts to waste yarn, move leg sts to another piece of waste yarn. Then move second set of 12 gusset sts to another piece of waste yarn. Using dpns, pick up and knit 1 st, pm, pick up and knit 1 st and knit the leg sts in the round.

Switch to C1, work in the round until leg measures 4 (5, 6, 7) in / 10 (12.5, 15, 18) cm from split.

Switch to smaller needles and work in K1, P1 Rib for 1 in / 2.5 cm.

Place sts from second leg on dpns and work as first.

Place gusset sts on separate dpns and use the Kitchener stitch to graft the gusset sts together.

Sleeves

Move 34 (35, 38, 40) sleeve sts to dpns.

Reattach C1 and knit around sleeve sts, pick up and knit 2 sts, pm, pick up and knit 2 sts—38 (39, 42, 44) sts.

Knit 5 rnds.

Dec Rnd: K1, k2tog, knit to last 3 sts before m, ssk, k1—2 sts decreased.

Rep this Dec Rnd every 4th rnd 3 (4, 5, 6) times more.

Work even until sleeve measures 4 (6, 7, 7) in / 10 (15, 18, 18) cm.

Switch to smaller needles and work K1, P1 Rib for 1 in / 2.5 cm. Bind off all sts in Rib pattern.

Back Flap

With C2, pick up 24 (26, 28, 30) sts.

Knit for 4 (4.5, 5, 6) in / 10 (11.5, 12.5, 15) cm, ending with a WS row. Cut yarn.

Turn piece and pick up 24 (26, 28, 36) sts along right side of flap, knit across 24 (26, 28, 30) sts at the top, pick up 24 (26, 28, 36) sts down the left side of the flap.

Work in K1, P1 Rib for 4 rows.

Buttonhole Row (WS): *P1, k1, yo, k2tog, p1, k1; rep from * to end.

Work K1, P1 Rib for 4 more rows. Bind off in Rib pattern.

Hood

With MC, carefully undo provisional CO and place sts on larger needles.

Next Row (WS): Purl.

Inc Row 1 (RS): K1 (6, 11, 12), *k1, k1fb; rep from * to last 1 (6, 11, 12) sts—66 (72, 72, 81) sts.

Next Row: Purl.

Inc Row 2: *K2, k1f&b; rep from * to end of row—88 (96, 96, 108) sts.

Work in St st until hood measures 7 (7, 7.5, 8) in / 18 (18, 19, 20.5) cm.

Using Kitchener stitch graft hood closed.

HOOD EDGING

With smaller needles and C1, beginning at right front edge after the button band, pick up and knit 2 sts for every 3 sts around the front, the hood, and the left front.

Ears (make 2)

With C1 and dpn(s), CO 16 sts, pm, and join to work in the rnd.

Knit 2 rnds.

Inc Rnd: *K1, k1f&b, k4, k1f&b, k1; rep from * once—20 sts.

Knit 1 rnd.

Inc Rnd: *K1, k1f&b, k6, k1f&b, k1; rep from * once—24 sts.

Knit 1 rnd.

Inc Rnd: *K1, k1f&b, k8, k1f&b, k1; rep from * once—28 sts.

Knit 1 rnd.

Dec Rnd: *K1, ssk, k8, k2tog, k1; rep from * once—24 sts.

Knit 1 rnd.

Dec Rnd: *K1, ssk, k6, k2tog, k1; rep from * once—20 sts.

Knit 1 rnd.

Dec Rnd: *K1, ssk, k4, k2tog, k1; rep from * once—16 sts.

Dec Rnd: *K1, ssk, k2, k2tog, k1; rep from * once—12 sts.

Dec Rnd: *K1, Ssk, k2tog, k1; rep from * once—8 sts.

Use Kitchener stitch to graft sts together.

Sew ears to the top of the hood on each side, using photos as a guide.

Mane

Using two strands of C2, and one strand each of MC and C1, make a 3 in / 7.5 cm pom-pom with 30 wraps. Carefully pull tight and leave a 12 in / 30.5 cm tail. Sew pom-pom securely to the top of the hood.

FINISHING

Sew buttons carefully on button band on opposite side matching buttonholes. Carefully sew buttons opposite buttonholes along bum flap.

Weave in all ends. Wash and block to measurements.

Elephant

You want to know a secret? This is the romper that started it all! Who doesn't want a little baby dressed up like an elephant? The end result was just so cute, I couldn't help myself and kept making sketches. It was like an endless dress-up clothes box that was only limited by my imagination. There are two versions of the elephant: a more realistic "Zoo Elephant" and one fit for a circus!

Sizes: Newborn (6 months, 12 months, 18 months)

Finished Chest Circumference: 16 (18, 20, 22) in / 40.5 (45.5, 51, 56) cm

Finished Head Circumference: 10.5 (12, 13.25, 14.5) in / 26.5 (30.5, 33.5, 37) cm

Gauge: 20 sts and 28 rows = 4 in / 10 cm in St st on larger needles

Yarn: The Fiber Seed, Sprout Worsted (#4 medium weight; 90% merino superwash wool, 10% nylon; 250 yd / 230 m per 4.8 oz / 136 g): 2 (2, 3, 3) skeins Elephant; for the Circus version, you will also need scrap yarn (less than 50 yd / 46 m) in your choice of colors

Needles: US 7 (4.5 mm) 16 in / 40 cm circular, or size needed to obtain gauge; US 5 (3.75 mm) 16 in /40 cm circular and dpn(s), or needles two sizes smaller than size needed to obtain gauge

Notions: Tapestry needle, three ½ in / 1.5 cm JHB buttons, 1 in / 2.5 cm wide snap tape, sewing needle and thread, waste yarn

Stitch Guide

K1, P1 RIB WORKED FLAT
Row 1: *K1, p1; rep from * to end of row.
Row 2: *P1, k1; rep from * to end of row.
Repeat Rows 1 and 2 for pattern.

K1, P1 RIB IN THE ROUND
Rnd 1: *K1, p1; rep from * to end of rnd.
Repeat Rnd 1 for pattern.

Seed Stitch
Row 1: *K1, p1; rep from * to end of row.
Row 2: *P1, k1; rep from * to end of row.
Repeat Rows 1 and 2 for pattern.

INSTRUCTIONS ZOO ELEPHANT

Body

With larger needles, cast on 49 (51, 55, 59) sts.

Set-up Row 1 (RS): K5 sts (button band), pm, k6 (6, 7, 7) front sts, pm, k6 (6, 7, 8) sleeve sts, pm, k15 (17, 17, 19) back sts, pm, k6 (6, 7, 8) sleeve sts, pm, k6 (6, 7, 7) front sts, pm, k5 sts (button band).

Set-up Row 2 (WS): K5, purl to last 5 sts, k5 (slipping all markers as you come to them).

Row 3 Increase Row (RS): K5, sm, *k to 1st before m, k1f&b, sm, k1f&b; rep from * 3 times, knit to end of row—53 (63, 69, 75) sts.

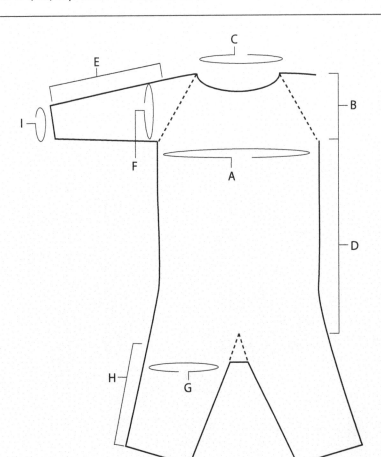

A - 16 (18, 20, 22) in
    40.5 (45.5, 51, 56) cm
B - 2.75 (3.5, 4, 4.5) in
    7 (9, 10, 11.5) cm
C - 9.75 (10.25, 11, 11.75) in
    25 (26, 28, 30) cm
D - 10.5 (13.5, 14.5, 15.5) in
    26.5 (34.5, 37, 39.5) cm
E - 7.5 (8.25, 9, 10) in
    19 (21, 23, 25.5) cm
F - 6 (6.75, 7.75, 8.75) in
    15 (17, 19.5, 22) cm
G - 8.25 (9, 9.75, 10.75) in
    21 (23, 25, 27.5) cm
H - 5.5 (6.5, 7.5, 8.5) in
    14 (16.5, 19, 21.5) cm
I - 4.75 (5.5, 6.5, 7.5) in
    12 (14, 16.5, 19) cm

Even Row (WS): K5, purl to last 5 sts, k5 (slipping all markers as you come to them).

Inc Row (RS): K5, sm, (knit to 1 st before m, k1f&b sm, k1f&b) 4 times, knit to end of row—57 (59, 63, 67) sts.

Even Row (WS): K5, purl to last 5 sts, k5 (slipping all markers as you come to them).

Buttonhole Inc Row (RS): K2, yo, k2tog, k1, sm, (knit to 1st before m, k1f&b, sm, k1f&b) 4 times, knit to end of row—65 (67, 71, 75) sts.

Even Row (WS): K5, purl to last 5 sts, k5 (slipping all markers as you come to them).

Inc Row (RS): K5, sm, (knit to 1 st before m, k1f&b sm, k1f&b) 4 times, knit to end of row—8 sts increased.

Repeat last two rows 2 (3, 4, 5) times more—89 (99, 111, 123) sts. Then work one more WS Even Row.

Buttonhole Inc Row (RS): K2, yo, k2tog, k1, sm, (knit to 1st before m, k1f&b, sm, k1f&b) 4 times, knit to end of row—97 (107, 119, 131) sts.

Even Row (WS): K5, purl to last 5 sts, k5 (slipping all markers as you come to them).

Inc Row (RS): K5, sm, (knit to 1 st before m, k1f&b sm, k1f&b) 4 times, knit to end of row—8 sts increased.

Repeat last two rows 1 (2, 3, 4) times more—113 (131, 151, 171) sts. Then work one more WS Even Row.

Buttonhole Inc Row (RS): K2, yo, k2tog, k1, sm, (knit to 1st before m, k1f&b, sm, k1f&b) 4 times, knit to end of row—121 (139, 159, 179) sts.

Even Row (WS): K5, purl to last 5 sts, k5 (slipping all markers as you come to them).

Joining Row (RS): K5, sm, (knit to 1 st before m, k1f&b sm, k1f&b) 4 times, knit to last 5 sts. Slip 5 sts purlwise from LH needle to spare dpn, then k2tog using 1 st from RH needle and 1 st from dpn five times—124 (142, 162, 182) sts.

Cut yarn, leaving a 12 in / 30.5 cm tail, slip 16 (18, 21, 23) sts purlwise to RH needle (all the sts before the first sleeve m).

Separate Sleeves: Remove m, then move 26 (30, 35, 40) sleeve sts to waste yarn, CO 2 sts, place new BOR m, CO 2 sts, remove m, knit to next m, remove m, move 26 (30, 35, 40) sleeve sts to waste yarn, CO 2 sts, pm, CO 2 sts, knit to end of rnd.

Knit every rnd until piece measures 10.5 (13.5, 14.5, 15.5) in / 26.5 (34.5, 37, 39.5) cm from underarm.

Gusset

Set-up Rnd 1: K19 (22, 24, 27) sts, place gusset m, k1, place gusset m, k39 (44, 49, 54) sts, place gusset m, k1, place gusset m, knit to end.

Set-up Rnd 2: Knit.

Gusset Inc Rnd: Knit to gusset m, sm, *m1L, knit to m, m1R, sm; rep from * once, knit to end.

Even Rnd: Knit.

Repeat last 2 rnds four times more, until there are 11 sts between the gusset markers.

Split Legs: Knit to last gusset m, slip next 11 sts to waste yarn, turn and purl back to the back gusset sts, slip next 11 sts to waste yarn. Continue working left leg only in St st flat, until leg measures 4 (5, 6, 7) in / 10 (12.5, 15, 18) cm from split.

Note: If preferred here, you can place the right leg sts on waste yarn or a holder, but you can easily leave them on the other portion of the circular needle while working the left leg flat.

Switch to smaller needles and work in k1, p1 rib for 1.5 in / 4 cm.

Gusset Snap Band: With smaller needles and RS facing and starting at the bottom right corner of the front above the Rib stitch, pick up and knit 2 sts for every 3 sts along the

leg, move the 11 held gusset sts on to spare needles and knit across, pick up and knit 2 sts for every 3 sts along the leg. Knit every row for 1.5" [4 cm]. Bind off all sts. Repeat for back side.

Sleeves

Move 26 (30, 35, 40) sleeve sts to dpns.

Reattach yarn and knit around sleeve sts, pick up and knit 2 sts, pm, pick up and knit 2 sts—30 (34, 39, 44) sts.

Knit 3 rnds.

Dec Rnd: K1, k2tog, knit to last 3 sts before m, ssk, k1—28 (32, 37, 42) sts.

Knit 10 (10, 12, 14) rnds.

Dec Rnd: K1, k2tog, knit to last 3 sts before m, ssk, k1—26 (30, 35, 40) sts.

Knit 10 (10, 12, 14) rnds.

Dec Rnd: K1, k2tog, knit to last 3 sts before m, ssk, k1—24 (28, 33, 38) sts.

Knit until sleeve measures 5.5 (6.25, 7, 8) in / 14 (16, 18, 20.5) cm from underarm.

Final Dec Rnd (Size 12 Month Only): K1, k2tog, knit to end—24 (28, 32, 38) sts.

Switch to smaller needles and work in K1, P1 Rib for 2 in / 5 cm. Bind off all sts in Rib pattern.

NECK EDGING

With smaller needles, starting at the right front edge immediately following the button band, pick up and knit 34 (42, 50, 56) sts.

Work in K1, P1 Rib for 3 Rows. Bind off all sts in Rib pattern.

Tail

With MC and dpn(s), and using photos as a guide, pick up and knit 3 sts from back of romper. *Knit the 3 sts across the dpn, from the left needle to the right needle. Then, slide the sts from one end of the needle to the other, while holding the tail in back, repeat from * until I-cord is 2 in / 5 cm. Cut three 1 in / 2.5 cm strands of yarn, hold at end of I-cord, cut yarn, pull tight, and tie around the middle of the three strands.

FINISHING

Sew snap tape on the gusset band. Weave in all ends. Wash and block.

Sew buttons opposite buttonholes on front button bands.

CIRCUS ELEPHANT

Body

With MC and larger needles, cast on 45 (53, 61, 67) sts.

Row 1 (RS): K5 sts (button band), pm, k5 (7, 8, 9) front sts, pm, k5 (6, 7, 8) sleeve sts, pm, k15 (19, 21, 23) back sts, pm, k5 (6, 7, 8) sleeve sts, pm, k5 (7, 8, 9) front sts, pm, k5 sts (button band).

Row 2 (WS): K5, purl to last 5 sts, k5 (slipping all markers as you come to them).

Row 3 Increase Row (RS): K5, sm, *k to 1st before m, kf/, sm, k1f&b; rep from * 3 times, knit to end of row—8 sts increased.

Row 4 (WS): K5, purl to last 5 sts, k5 (slipping all markers as you come to them).

Row 5 Increase Row and Buttonhole (RS): K2, yo, k2tog, k1, sm, *k to 1st before m, k1f&b, sm, k1f&b; rep from * 3 times, knit to end of row—8 sts increased.

Row 6 (WS): K5, purl to last 5 sts, k5 (slipping all markers as you come to them).

Row 7 Increase Row (RS): K5, sm, *k to 1st before m, k1f&b, sm, k1f&b; rep from * 3 times, knit to end of row—8 sts increased.

Repeat last two rows 2 (3, 4, 4) times more.

Row 8 (WS): K5, purl to last 5 sts, k5 (slipping all markers as you come to them).

Row 9 Increase Row and Buttonhole (RS): K2, yo, k2tog, k1, sm, *k to 1st before m, k1f&b, sm, k1f&b; rep from * 3 times, knit to end of row—8 sts increased.

Row 10 (WS): K5, purl to last 5 sts, k5 (slipping all markers as you come to them).

Row 11 Increase Row (RS): K5, sm, *k to 1st before m, kf/, sm, k1f&b; rep from * 3 times, knit to end of row—8 sts increased.

Row 12 (WS): K5, purl to last 5 sts, k5 (slipping all markers as you come to them).

Work last 2 rows 2 (2, 3, 4) times more.

Row 13 Increase Row and Buttonhole (RS): K2, yo, k2tog, k1, sm, *k to 1st before m, k1f&b, sm, k1f&b; rep from * 3 times, knit to end of row—8 sts increased.

Row 14 (WS): K5, purl to last 5 sts, k5 (slipping all markers as you come to them).

Joining Row (RS): K5, sm, k to 1st before m, k1f&b, sm, k1f&b; rep from * 3 times, knit to last 5 sts, move the 5 sts from Left needle to a spare needle, hold to back and k2tog with the 5 button band sts from Right needle—8 sts increased.

Separate Sleeves and Gusset

Rnd 1: Knit.

Rnd 2: Knit to 1 m, remove m, move 31 (32, 33, 36) sleeve sts to waste yarn, CO 1 st, pm (this will also serve as your start of rnd m), CO 1 st, remove m, knit to next m, remove m, move 31 (32, 33, 36) sleeve sts to waste yarn, CO 1 st, pm, CO 1 st, knit to end of rnd.

Knit until piece measures 10.5 (13.5, 14.5, 15.5) in / 26.5 (34.5, 37, 39.5cm from CO edge.

Rnd 3: *K19 (22, 24, 30) sts, place gusset m, k1, place gusset m, k19 (22, 24, 30) sts; rep from * once.

Rnd 4: Sm, *knit to m, sm, m1L, k1, m1R, sm, knit to m, sm; rep from * once.

Rnd 5: Knit.

Rnd 6: Knit.

Repeat last 2 rnds, until there are 11 sts between the gusset markers.

Rnd 7: Knit.

Rnd 8: Knit to gusset m, remove m, move the next 11 sts to waste yarn, turn, purl to next gusset m, move the 11 gusset sts to scrap yarn, turn.

Knit the remaining sts on the needles until the piece measures 5 (6, 8, 9) in / 12.5 (15, 20.5, 23) cm from leg separation.

Switch to smaller needles and work in Seed st for 1.5 in / 4 cm.

Sleeves

Move 31 (32, 33, 36) sleeve sts to dpns.

Rnd 1: Reattach yarn and knit around sleeve sts, pick up and knit 2 sts, pm, pick up and knit 1 sts.

Rnds 2-4: Knit.

Rnd 5 Dec Rnd: K1, k2tog, knit to last 3 sts before m, ssk, k1.

Knit 10 (10, 12, 14) rnds.

Rnd 6 Dec Rnd: K1, k2tog, knit to last 3 sts before m, ssk, k1.

Knit 10 (10, 12, 14) rnds.

Rnd 7 Dec Rnd: K1, k2tog, knit to last 3 sts before m, ssk, k1.

Knit until sleeve measures 4.5 (5, 6, 7) in / 11.5 (12.5, 15, 18) cm from underarm.

Switch to smaller needles and work in Seed st for 1 in / 2.5 cm.

Gusset Snap Band: With smaller needles and with RS facing, start at the bottom right pick up and knit 2 sts for every 3 sts along the leg, move the 11 held sts on to spare needles and knit across, pick up and knit 2 sts for every 3 sts along the leg. Work in Garter st for 6 rows. Bind off all sts.

Repeat for second side.

Collar

With smaller needles and CC, starting at the right front edge immediately following the button band, pick up and knit 34 (42, 50, 56) sts.

Row 1: *K1f&b; rep from * to end of row.

Row 2: Purl.

Row 3: Knit.

Row 4: Purl.

Row 5: Knit.

Row 6: Purl.

Row 7: Knit.

Row 8: *P2tog; rep from * to end of row.

Row 9: Switch to CC2 *K1f&b; rep from * to end of row.

Row 10: Purl.

Row 11: Knit.

Row 12: Purl.

Row 13: Knit.

Row 14: Purl.

Row 15: *K2tog, suspended bind off.

Tail

With MC and dpn(s), and using photos as a guide, pick up and knit 3 sts from back of romper. *Knit the 3 sts across the dpn, from the left needle to the right needle. Then, slide the sts from one end of the needle to the other, while holding the tail in back, repeat from * until I-cord is 2 in / 5 cm. Cut three, 1 in / 2.5 cm strands of yarn, hold at end of I-cord, cut yarn, pull tight, and tie around the middle of the three strands.

FINISHING

Sew snap tape on the gusset band. Weave in all ends. Wash and block.

Sew buttons opposite buttonholes on front button bands.

Hat (Both Versions)

With MC and larger needles, cast on 56 (64, 72, 80) sts, place marker and join in the round, being careful not to twist stitches.

Rnds 1-8: *K1, p1; rep from * to end of rnd.

Knit for 5.5 in / 14 cm.

CROWN SHAPING

Switch to DPNs when necessary.

Rnd 1: *K6, k2tog; repeat from * around—49 (56, 63, 70) sts.

Rnds 2-4: Knit all sts.

Rnd 5: *K5, k2tog; repeat from * around—42 (48, 54, 60) sts.

Rnds 6-7: Knit all sts.

Rnd 8: *K4, k2tog; repeat from * around—35 (40, 45, 50) sts.

Rnd 9: Knit all sts.

Rnd 10: *K3, k2tog; repeat from * around—28 (32, 36, 40) sts.

Rnd 11: *K2, k2tog; repeat from * around—21 (24, 27, 30) sts.

Rnd 12: Switch to MC and Knit 1 Row.

Rnd 13: *K1, k2tog; repeat from * around—14 (16, 18, 20) sts.

Rnd 14: *K2tog; repeat from * around—7 (8, 9, 10) sts.

Cut yarn and thread through remaining live stitches. Pull tightly and secure. Weave in all loose ends.

Ears

Using photos as a guide, pick up and knit 8 sts along the side, then pick up the 8 sts exactly parallel to those 8 sts. Reattach yarn, pm, and begin to work in the round.

Rnds 1-3: Knit.

Rnd 4: *K1f&b, k6, k1f&b; rep from * once—20 sts.

Rnd 5: Knit.

Rnd 6: *K1f&b, k8, k1f&b; rep from * once—24 sts.

Rnd 7: Knit.

Rnd 8: *K1f&b, k10, k1f&b; rep from * once—28 sts.

Rnd 9: Knit.

Rnd 10: *K1f&b, k12, k1f&b; rep from * once—32 sts.

Rnd 11: Knit.

Rnd 12: *K1f&b, k14, k1f&b; rep from * once—36 sts.

Rnds 13-18: Knit.

Rnd 19: *Ssk, k14, k2tog; rep from * once—32 sts.

Rnd 20: Knit.

Rnd 21: *Ssk, k12, k2tog; rep from * once—28 sts.

Rnd 22-24: Knit.

Use Kitchener stitch to graft the remaining stitches together.

Trunk

Cast on 20 sts, leaving a long tail for attaching to hat later.

Join and knit in rnd in St st for 5 in / 12.5 cm.

Cut yarn, pull tight through all sts to close hole.

Using the long cast-on tail, whipstitch to front of hat, using photos as a guide.

FINISHING

Sew two large black buttons on either side of hat for eyes.

Weave in ends and block.

Panda

In one of our favorite read-alouds—*The Vanderbeekers of 141st Street* by Karina Yan Glaser—the little Vanderbeeker loves to pretend that she's a panda. I may have used this fun book a few times during the writing of *this* book so that my own children would be entertained and safely contained in my office. Since this story became such a part of getting this book done, I couldn't leave out the panda, now, could I? When you finish this sweet little romper, you'll have a Panda of your very own!

Sizes: Newborn (6 months, 12 months, 18 months)

Finished Chest Circumference: 16 (18, 20, 22) in / 40.5 (45.5, 51, 56) cm

Gauge: 20 sts and 28 rows = 4 in / 10 cm in St st on larger needles

Yarn: Knit Picks, Shine Worsted (#4 medium weight; 60% pima cotton, 40% Modal; 75 yd / 69 m per 1.75 oz / 50 g): 3 (3, 4, 5) skeins White (MC) and 2 (2, 3, 3) skeins Black (C1)

Needles: US 7 (4.5 mm) 16 in / 40 cm circular, or size needed to obtain gauge; US 5 (3.75 mm) 16 in /40 cm circular and dpn(s), or needles two sizes smaller than size needed to obtain gauge

Notions: Tapestry needle, 1 in / 2.5 cm wide snap tape, sewing needle and thread, waste yarn

Stitch Guide

K1, P1 RIB WORKED FLAT
Row 1: *K1, p1; rep from * to end of row.
Row 2: *P1, k1; rep from * to end of row.
Repeat Rows 1 and 2 for pattern.

K1, P1 RIB IN THE ROUND
Rnd 1: *K1, p1; rep from * to end of rnd.
Repeat Rnd 1 for pattern.

INSTRUCTIONS

Body

With MC and larger needles, CO 47 (55, 59, 67) sts.

Set-up Row 1 (RS): K5 sts (button band), pm, k6 (7, 8, 9) front sts, pm, k5 (6, 7, 8) sleeve sts, pm, k15 (19, 19, 23) back sts, pm, k5 (6, 7, 8) sleeve sts, pm, k6 (7, 8, 9) front sts, pm, k5 sts (button band).

Set-up Row 2 (WS): K5, purl to last 5 sts, k5 (slipping all markers as you come to them).

Inc Row (RS): K5, sm, (knit to 1 st before m, k1f&b sm, k1f&b) 4 times, knit to end of row—55 (63, 67, 75) sts.

Even Row (WS): K5, purl to last 5 sts, k5 (slipping all markers as you come to them).

Buttonhole Inc Row (RS): K2, yo, k2tog, k1, sm, (knit to 1st before m, k1f&b, sm, k1f&b) 4 times, knit to end of row—63 (71, 75, 83) sts.

Even Row (WS): K5, purl to last 5 sts, k5 (slipping all markers as you come to them).

Inc Row (RS): K5, sm, (knit to 1 st before m, k1f&b sm, k1f&b) 4 times, knit to end of row—8 sts increased.

Repeat last two rows 2 (3, 4, 4) times more—87 (103, 115, 123) sts.

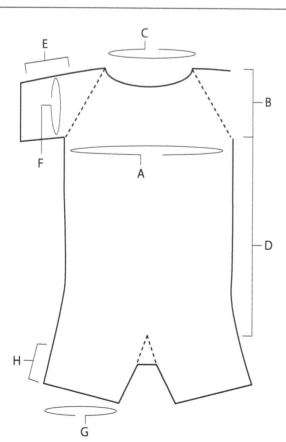

A - 16 (18, 20, 22) in 40.5 (45.5, 51, 56) cm
B - 3.25 (3.5, 4, 4.25) in 8.5 (9, 10, 11) cm
C - 9.5 (11, 11.75, 13.5) in 24 (28, 30, 34.5) cm
D - 10.5 (13.5, 14.5, 15.5) in 26.5 (34.5, 37, 39.5) cm
E - 2.5 in / 5 cm
F - 6 (6.5, 7.5, 8.25) in 15 (16.5, 19, 21) cm
G - 9.5 (10.5, 11.5, 12.5) in 24 (26.5, 29, 32) cm
H - 3.5 (3.5, 4.5, 4.5) in 9 (9, 11.5, 11.5) cm

Then work one more WS Even Row.

Buttonhole Inc Row (RS): K2, yo, k2tog, k1, sm, (knit to 1st before m, k1f&b, sm, k1f&b) 4 times, knit to end of row—95 (111, 123, 131) sts.

Even Row (WS): K5, purl to last 5 sts, k5 (slipping all markers as you come to them).

Inc Row (RS): K5, sm, (knit to 1 st before m, k1f&b sm, k1f&b) 4 times, knit to end of row—8 sts increased.

Repeat last two rows 2 (2, 3, 4) times more—119 (135, 155, 171) sts.

Then work one more WS Even Row.

Buttonhole Inc Row (RS): K2, yo, k2tog, k1, sm, (knit to 1st before m, k1f&b, sm, k1f&b) 4 times, knit to end of row—127 (143, 163, 179) sts.

Even Row (WS): K5, purl to last 5 sts, k5 (slipping all markers as you come to them).

Joining Row (RS): K5, sm, (knit to 1 st before m, k1f&b sm, k1f&b) 4 times, knit to last 5 sts. Slip 5 sts purlwise from the LH needle to spare dpn, then k2tog using 1 st from the RH needle and 1 st from dpn five times—130 (146, 166, 182) sts.

Knit 1 rnd.

Separate Sleeves: Remove m, then knit to next m, move 27 (30, 35, 38) sleeve sts to waste yarn, CO 1 st, place new BOR m, CO 1 st, remove m, knit to next m, remove m, move 27 (30, 35, 38) sleeve sts to waste yarn, CO 1 st, pm, CO 1 st, knit to end of rnd.

Knit every rnd until piece measures 10.5 (13.5, 14.5, 15.5) in / 26.5 (34.5, 37, 39.5) cm from underarm.

Gusset

Set-up Rnd 1: K19 (22, 24, 27) sts, place gusset m, k1, place gusset m, k39 (44, 49, 54) sts, place gusset m, k1, place gusset m, knit to end.

Set-up Rnd 2: Knit.

Gusset Inc Rnd: Knit to gusset m, sm, *m1L, knit to m, m1R, sm; rep from * once, knit to end.

Even Rnd: Knit.

Repeat last 2 rnds four times more, until there are 11 sts between the gusset markers.

Split Legs: Knit to last gusset m, slip next 11 sts to waste yarn, turn and purl back to the back gusset sts, slip next 11 sts to waste yarn. Switch to CC and continue working left leg only in St st flat, until leg measures 2 (2, 3, 3) in / 5 (5, 7.5, 7.5) cm from split.

Note: If preferred here, you can place the right leg sts on waste yarn or a holder, but you can easily leave them on the other portion of the circular needle while working the left leg flat.

Switch to smaller needles and work in K1, P1 Rib for 1.5 in / 4 cm.

Gusset Snap Band: With MC and smaller needles, with RS facing and starting at the bottom right corner of the front above the Rib stitch, pick up and knit 2 sts for every 3

FRONT

BACK

sts along the leg, move the 11 held gusset sts on to spare needles and knit across, pick up and knit 2 sts for every 3 sts along the leg. Knit every row for 1.5 in / 4 cm. Bind off all sts. Repeat for back side.

Sleeves

Move 27 (30, 35, 38) sleeve sts to dpns.
Reattach yarn and knit around sleeve sts, pick up and knit 2 sts, pm, pick up and knit 1 st—30 (33, 38, 41) sts.
Knit 3 rnds.
Switch to CC and knit 1 rnd.
Switch to smaller needles and work in K1, P1 Rib for 1.5 in / 4 cm. Bind off all sts in Rib pattern.

NECK EDGING

With smaller needles and CC, starting at the back of the neck, pick up and knit 2 sts for every 3 sts around neck edge. Bind off all sts purlwise.

Eyes (Make 2)

With CC, CO 3 sts.
Row 1: K1f&b, k1, k1f&b—5 sts.
Row 2: Purl.
Work in St st for 2 rows.
Row 5: SSk, k1, k2tog—3 sts.
Bind off all sts purl wise, leaving a 12 in / 30.5 cm tail.

Nose

CO 6 sts.
Work in St st for 2 in / 5 cm.
Bind off all sts knitwise, leaving a 12 in / 30.5 cm tail.

FINISHING

Using photos as a guide, sew eyes and nose to the front of romper.
Sew buttons carefully on button band on opposite side matching buttonholes.
Using a sewing machine, or needle and thread, carefully sew snap tape along the RS of the gusset snap band.
Weave in all ends. Wash and block to measurements.

Penguin

My middle child used to absolutely love penguins (one of his favorite shows had a penguin character that rescued all kinds of sea creatures). For about a year, we looked for penguins everywhere, and he would light up with glee whenever he saw one. We had all kinds of penguins, but I'd never had a sweet baby penguin of my own to cuddle—until now. Once you knit up this little romper, you'll have a penguin of your own, too.

Sizes: Newborn (6 months, 12 months, 18 months)

Finished Chest Circumference: 16 (18, 20, 22) in / 40.5 (45.5, 51, 56) cm

Gauge: 20 sts and 28 rows = 4 in / 10 cm in St st on larger needles

Yarn: Knit One Crochet Too, Nautika (#4 medium weight; 85% microfiber acrylic, 15% nylon; 98 yd / 90 m per 1.75 oz / 50 g): 3 (3, 4, 4) skeins #900 Ebony (MC); 1 (1, 1, 1) skein #100 Snow (C1); and 1 (1, 1, 1) skein #372 Tangerine (C2)

Needles: US 7 (4.5 mm) 16 in / 40 cm circular, or size needed to obtain gauge; US 5 (3.75 mm) 16 in / 40 cm circular and dpn(s), or needles two sizes smaller than size needed to obtain gauge

Notions: Tapestry needle, 1 in / 2.5 cm wide snap tape, sewing needle and thread, waste yarn

Stitch Guide

K1, P1 RIB WORKED FLAT

Row 1: *K1, p1; rep from * to end of row.
Row 2: *P1, k1; rep from * to end of row.
Repeat Rows 1 and 2 for pattern.

K1, P1 RIB IN THE ROUND

Rnd 1: *K1, p1; rep from * to end of rnd.
Repeat Rnd 1 for pattern.

INSTRUCTIONS

Body

With MC, and larger needles, CO 47 (55, 59, 67) sts.

Set-up Row 1 (RS): K5 sts (button band), pm, k6 (7, 8, 9) back sts, pm, k5 (6, 7, 8) sleeve sts, pm, switch to C1 and k15 (19, 19, 23) front sts, pm, switch to a second ball of MC and k5 (6, 7, 8) sleeve sts, pm, k6 (7, 8, 9) back sts, pm, k5 sts (button band). (Note: You will work the front sts in C1 only until after the sleeve split).

Set-up Row 2 (WS): K5, purl to last 5 sts, k5 (slipping all markers as you come to them).

Inc Row (RS): K5, sm, (knit to 1 st before m, k1f&b sm, k1f&b) 4 times, knit to end of row— 55 (63, 67, 75) sts.

Even Row (WS): K5, purl to last 5 sts, k5 (slipping all markers as you come to them).

Buttonhole Inc Row (RS): K2, yo, k2tog, k1, sm, (knit to 1st before m, k1f&b, sm, k1f&b) 4 times, knit to end of row—63 (71, 75, 83) sts.

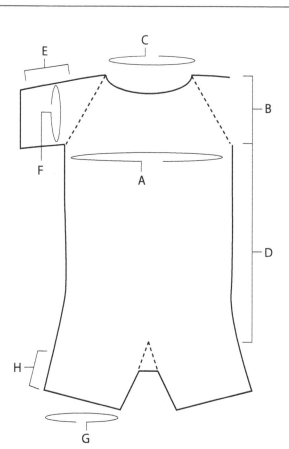

A - 16 (18, 20, 22) in
    40.5 (45.5, 51, 56) cm
B - 3.25 (3.5, 4, 4.25) in
    8.5 (9, 10, 11) cm
C - 9.5 (11, 11.75, 13.5) in
    24 (28, 30, 34.5) cm
D - 10.5 (13.5, 14.5, 15.5) in
    26.5 (34.5, 37, 39.5) cm
E - 2.5 in / 5 cm
F - 6 (6.5, 7.5, 8.25) in
    15 (16.5, 19, 21) cm
G - 9.5 (10.5, 11.5, 12.5) in
    24 (26.5, 29, 32) cm
H - 3.5 (3.5, 4.5, 4.5) in
    9 (9, 11.5, 11.5) cm

Even Row (WS): K5, purl to last 5 sts, k5 (slipping all markers as you come to them).

Inc Row (RS): K5, sm, (knit to 1 st before m, k1f&b sm, k1f&b) 4 times, knit to end of row—8 sts increased.

Repeat last two rows 2 (3, 4, 4) times more—87 (103, 115, 123) sts.

Then work one more WS Even Row.

Buttonhole Inc Row (RS): K2, yo, k2tog, k1, sm, (knit to 1st before m, k1f&b, sm, k1f&b) 4 times, knit to end of row—95 (111, 123, 131) sts.

Even Row (WS): K5, purl to last 5 sts, k5 (slipping all markers as you come to them).

Inc Row (RS): K5, sm, (knit to 1 st before m, k1f&b sm, k1f&b) 4 times, knit to end of row—8 sts increased.

Repeat last two rows 2 (2, 3, 4) times more—119 (135, 155, 171) sts.

Then work one more WS Even Row.

Buttonhole Inc Row (RS): K2, yo, k2tog, k1, sm, (knit to 1st before m, k1f&b, sm, k1f&b) 4 times, knit to end of row—127 (143, 163, 179) sts.

Even Row (WS): K5, purl to last 5 sts, k5 (slipping all markers as you come to them).

Joining Row (RS): *Using MC only across all sts,* k5, sm, (knit to 1 st before m, k1f&b sm, k1f&b) 4 times, knit to last 5 sts. Slip 5 sts purlwise from the LH needle to spare dpn, then k2tog

using 1 st from RH needle and 1 st from dpn five times—130 (146, 166, 182) sts.

Knit 1 rnd.

Separate Sleeves: Remove m, then knit to next m, move 27 (30, 35, 38) sleeve sts to waste yarn, CO 1 st, place new BOR m, CO 1 st, remove m, knit to next m, remove m, move 27 (30, 35, 38) sleeve sts to waste yarn, CO 1 st, pm, CO 1 st, knit to end of rnd.

Knit every rnd until piece measures 10.5 (13.5, 14.5, 15.5) in / 26.5 (34.5, 37, 39.5) cm from underarm.

Gusset

Set-up Rnd 1: K19 (22, 24, 27) sts, place gusset m, k1, place gusset m, k39 (44, 49, 54) sts, place gusset m, k1, place gusset m, knit to end.

Set-up Rnd 2: Knit.

Gusset Inc Rnd: Knit to gusset m, sm, *m1L, knit to m, m1R, sm; rep from * once, knit to end.

Even Rnd: Knit.

Repeat last 2 rnds four times more, until there are 11 sts between the gusset markers.

Split Legs: Knit to last gusset m, slip next 11 sts to waste yarn, turn and purl back to the back gusset sts, slip next 11 sts to waste yarn. Work 2 rows in St st. Switch to C2 and continue working left leg only in St st flat, until leg

FRONT

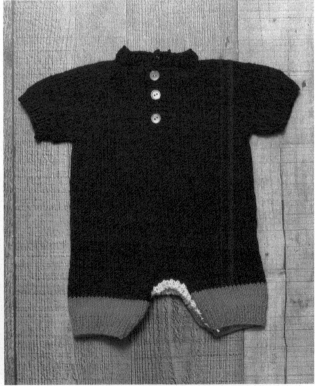

BACK

measures 2 (2, 3, 3) in / 5 (5, 7.5, 7.5) cm from split.

Note: If preferred here, you can place the right leg sts on waste yarn or a holder, but you can easily leave them on the other portion of the circular needle while working the left leg flat.

Switch to smaller needles and work in K1, P1 Rib for 1.5 in / 4 cm.

Gusset Snap Band: With smaller needles and C1 and RS facing and starting at the bottom right corner of the front above the Rib stitch, pick up and knit 2 sts for every 3 sts along the leg, move the 11 held gusset sts on to spare needles and knit across, pick up and knit 2 sts for every 3 sts along the leg. Knit every row for 1.5 in / 4 cm. Bind off all sts. Repeat for back side.

Sleeves

Move 27 (30, 35, 38) sleeve sts to dpns.

Reattach MC and knit around sleeve sts, pick up and knit 2 sts, pm, pick up and knit 1 st—30 (33, 38, 41) sts.

Knit 4 rnds.

Switch to smaller needles and work in K1, P1 Rib for 1.5 in / 4 cm. Bind off all sts in Rib pattern.

NECK EDGING

With smaller needles and MC, starting at the back of the neck, pick up and knit 2 sts for every 3 sts around neck edge.

Work in K1, P1 Rib for 3 rows. Bind off all sts in Rib pattern.

FINISHING

Sew buttons carefully on button band on opposite side matching buttonholes.

Using a sewing machine, or needle and thread, carefully sew snap tape along the RS of the gusset snap band.

Weave in all ends. Wash and block to measurements.

Flamingo

I wasn't really thinking about making a flamingo, until my youngest became a huge fan of this adorable show that has a flamingo and penguin deliver baby animals to their forever families. Yes, I became quite hooked on this one pretty fast, and did a lot of knitting for this book while watching. Suddenly, I just knew I needed a bright pink flamingo!

Sizes: Newborn (3 months, 6 months, 9 months, 12 months, 18 months)

Finished Chest Circumference: 15 (16, 17, 18, 19, 20) in / 38 (40.5, 43, 45.5, 48.5, 51) cm

Gauge: 20 sts and 28 rows = 4 in / 10 cm in St st on larger needles

Yarn: Fibre Art Studio, SW Merino Worsted (#4 medium weight; 100% superwash merino; 220 yd / 200 m per 3.5 oz / 100 g): 1 (1, 1, 1, 1, 1) skein Cotton Candy (MC) and 1 (1, 1, 1, 1, 1) skein Girl's Dream (CC)

Needles: US 6 (4.0 mm) 16 in / 40 cm circular, or size needed to obtain gauge

Notions: Tapestry needle, 1 in / 2.5 cm wide snap tape, sewing needle and thread

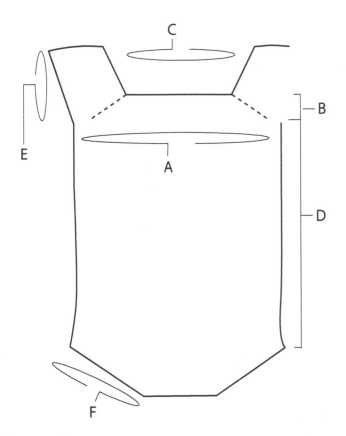

A - 15 (16, 17, 18, 19, 20) in
   38 (40.5, 43, 45.5, 48.5, 51) cm
B - 1.5 (1.5, 1.75, 1.75, 2, 2) in
   4 (4, 4.5, 4.5, 5, 5) cm
C - 13 (13.25, 14.5, 15.5, 15.75, 16.75) in
   33 (33.5, 37, 39.5, 40, 42.5) cm
D - 6 (6.5, 7, 8, 8.5, 9) in
   15 (16.5, 18, 20.5, 21.5, 23) cm
E - 5.25 (5.25, 6, 6.5, 6.75, 7.25) in
   13.5 (13.5, 15, 16.5, 17, 18.5) cm
F - 7.5 (7.25, 8, 8.25, 9.25, 9) in
   19 (18.5, 20.5, 21, 23.5, 23) cm

INSTRUCTIONS

Body

With MC, CO 65 (66, 73, 78, 79, 84) sts, pm, and join to work in the rnd, being careful not to twist your sts.

Set-up Rnd: K16 (16, 18, 20, 20, 22) sleeve sts, pm, k17 (17, 19, 19, 20, 20) back sts, pm, k16 (16, 18, 20, 20, 22) sleeve sts, pm, k16 (17, 18, 19, 19, 20) front sts.

Next Rnd: Knit.

Inc Rnd: (K1f&b, knit to 1 st before m, k1f&b, sm) 4 times—8 sts increased.

Even Rnd: Knit.

Repeat last two rnds 4 (4, 5, 5, 6, 6) times more—105 (106, 121, 126, 135, 140) sts.

Next Rnd (Create Shoulders): Remove m, bind off 26 (26, 30, 32, 34, 36) sleeve sts, remove m, knit across 27 (27, 31, 31, 34, 34) back sts, remove m, bind off 26 (26, 30, 32, 34, 36) sleeve sts, remove m, then knit across 26 (27, 30, 31, 33, 34) front sts.

Underarm Rnd: CO 6 (6, 6, 7, 7, 8) sts, place new BOR m, CO 5 (7, 6, 7, 7, 8) knit across 27 (27, 31, 31, 34, 34) back sts, bind off 26 (26, 30, 32, 34, 46) sleeve sts, remove m, using the backwards loop cast-on, CO 11 (13, 12, 14, 14, 16) sts, knit across 26 (27, 30, 31, 33, 34) front sts, knit to end of rnd.

Knit every rnd until piece measures 2 (2.5, 2.5, 3, 3.5, 4) in / 5 (6.5, 6.5, 7.5, 9, 10) cm from underarm.

Inc Rnd: *K4, k1f&b; rep form * to end of rnd—90 (96, 102, 108, 114, 120) sts.

Continue to knit in the rnd until piece measures 6.5 (6.5, 7, 8, 8.5, 9) in / 16.5 (16.5, 18, 20.5, 21.5, 23) cm.

Back Shaping

Row 1 (RS): Bind off 8 (8, 8, 9, 10, 10) sts, k37 (40, 43, 45, 49, 52) sts. Place remaining 45 (48, 51, 54, 57, 60) sts on hold for front.

Row 2 (WS): Bind off 8 (8, 8, 9, 10, 10) sts, purl to end—29 (32, 35, 36, 37, 40) sts.

Work 6 (4, 0, 2, 2, 0) rows in flat St st.

Dec Row (RS): K1, ssk, knit to last 3 sts, k2tog, k1—2 sts decreased.

Even Row (WS): Purl.

Repeat last 2 rows 3 (4, 5, 5, 5, 6) times more—21 (22, 23, 24, 25, 26) sts.

Work in flat St st for 5 (5, 5, 5, 7, 7) rows. Bind off all sts.

FRONT

BACK

Front Shaping

Row 1 (RS): Bind off 10 (10, 12, 12, 14, 14) sts, knit to end.

Row 2 (WS): Bind off 10 (10, 12, 12, 14, 14) sts, purl to end—25 (28, 27, 30, 29, 32) sts.

Work 4 (0, 6, 2, 8, 4) rows in flat St st.

Dec Row (RS): K1, ssk, knit to last 3 sts, k2tog, k1—2 sts decreased.

Even Row (WS): Purl.

Repeat last 2 rows 2 (3, 2, 3, 2, 3) times more— 19 (20, 21, 22, 23, 24) sts. Bind off all sts.

ARM EDGING

With CC, pick up 2 sts for every 3 sts around armhole. Bind off all sts.

LEG EDGING

With CC, pick up 2 sts for every 3 sts around leg opening. **Inc Rnd:** *P1f&b; rep from * around.

Next Rnd: Knit.

Next Rnd: Purl.

Bind off all sts knitwise.

NECK EDGING

With CC, pick up sts along neck edging (1 st for every neck st). Bind off all sts.

Feather Ruffles

With CC, and the back facing, pick up 10 sts about 6.5 in / 16.5 cm from the bottom edge.

Next Row: Purl.

Inc Row: *K1f&b; rep from * to end of row.

Work in St st for 1 in / 2.5 cm.

Bind off all sts knitwise.

Two rows under the first ruffle, with CC, pick up and knit 20 sts.

Next Row: Purl.

Inc Row: *K1f&b; rep from * to end of row.

Work in St st for 2 in / 5 cm.

Bind off all sts knitwise.

Three rows under second ruffle, with CC, pick up and knit 30 sts.

Next Row: Purl.

Inc Row: *K1, k1f&b; rep form * to end of row.

Work in St st for 3 in / 7.5 cm.

Bind off all sts knitwise.

FINISHING

Weave in all ends. Wash and block as desired.

Sew snap tape on opposite sides of bottom flaps.

MOMMY'S *Little Monkey*

One of my favorite animals—ever—has always been the monkey! I think it has to do with a childhood filled with books about a certain curious monkey and his friend with a yellow hat. My children have often reminded me of little monkeys—climbing everything they shouldn't, getting into all sorts of mischief, stealing bananas, and just bringing smiles wherever they go. Although this romper is simple to make, it still might be one of my favorite pieces in the whole book. It's timeless, it's classic, and it is just oh-so-cute.

Sizes: Newborn (6 months, 12 months, 18 months)

Finished Chest Circumference: 16 (18, 20, 22) in / 40.5 (45.5, 48.5, 51) cm

Finished Head Circumference: 10.5 (12, 13.25, 14.5) in / 26.5 (30.5, 33.5, 37) cm

Gauge: 24 sts and 32 rows = 4 in / 10 cm in St st on larger needles

Yarn: SweetGeorgia Yarns, Superwash DK (#3 light weight; 100% superwash merino; 256 yd / 234 m per 4 oz / 115 g): 2 (2, 3, 3) skeins Walnut (MC) and 1 (1, 1, 1) skein Tumbled Stone (CC)

Needles: US 6 (4.0 mm) 16 in / 40 cm circular, or size needed to obtain gauge; US 4 (3.5 mm) 16 in / 40 cm circular and dpn(s), or needles two sizes smaller than size needed to obtain gauge

Notions: Tapestry needle, three ½ in / 1.5 cm JHB buttons, 1 in / 2.5 cm wide snap tape, sewing needle and thread, waste yarn

Stitch Guide

K1, P1 RIB WORKED FLAT

Row 1: *K1, p1; rep from * to end of row.

Row 2: *P1, k1; rep from * to end of row.

Repeat Rows 1 and 2 for pattern.

K1, P1 IN THE ROUND

Rnd 1: *K1, p1; rep from * to end of rnd.

Repeat Rnd 1 for pattern.

INSTRUCTIONS

With CC and smaller needles, CO 47 (51, 57, 63) sts.

Set-up Row 1 (RS): K11 (11, 13, 13) front sts, pm, k6 (6, 6, 8) sleeve sts, pm, k16 (20, 22, 24) back sts, pm, k6 (6, 6, 8) sleeve sts, pm, k8 (8, 10, 10) front sts.

Set-up Row 2 (WS): Knit.

Set-up Row 3: Knit.

Buttonhole Row (WS): Knit to last 3 sts, k2tog, yo, k1.

Switch to larger needles and MC.

Inc Row (RS): (Knit to 1 st before m, k1f&b, sm, k1f&b) 4 times, knit to end—55 (59, 65, 71) sts.

Even Row (WS): K3, purl to last 3 sts, k3 (slipping all markers as you come to them).

Next Inc Row (RS): (Knit to 1 st before m, k1f&b, sm, k1f&b) 4 times, knit to end—63 (67, 73, 79) sts.

Buttonhole Row (WS): K3, purl to last 3 sts, k2tog, yo, k1.

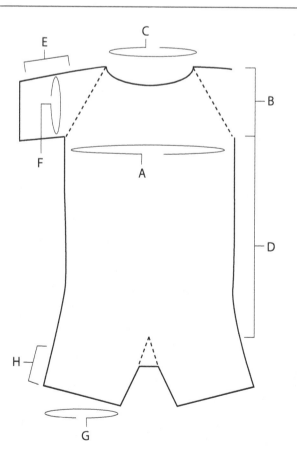

A - 16 (18, 19, 20) in
40.5 (45.5, 48.5, 51) cm

B - 3.75 (4.25, 4.25, 4.5) in
9.5 (11, 11, 11.5) cm

C - 7.75 (8.5, 9.5, 10.5) in
19.5 (21.5, 24, 26.5) cm

D - 10.5 (13.5, 14.5, 15.5) in
26.5 (34.5, 37, 39.5) cm

E - 1.5 (1.5, 1.25, 1.5) in
4 (4, 3, 4) cm

F - 6 (6.75, 7, 7.25) in
15 (17, 18, 18.5) cm

G - 9.25 (10.25, 10.75, 11.25) in
23.5 (26, 27.5, 28.5) cm

H - 3 (3.5, 3.75, 4) in
7.5 (9, 9.5, 10) cm

Next Inc Row (RS): (Knit to 1 st before m, k1f&b, sm, k1f&b) 4 times, knit to end—71 (75, 81, 87) sts.

Row 8: K3, purl to last 3 sts, k3.

Joining Rnd (RS): Slip 3 sts purlwise from RH needle to spare dpn, then k2tog using 1 st from RH needle and 1 st from dpn three times. Join to work in the round and place a different type of marker to distinguish the start of the round, (knit to 1 st before m, k1f&b, sm, k1f&b) 4 times, knit to end of rnd—76 (80, 86, 92) sts.

Even Rnd: Knit.

Inc Rnd: (Knit to 1 st before m, k1f&b, sm, k1f&b) 4 times, knit to end—84 (88, 94, 100) sts.

Repeat last 2 rnds 10 (12, 12, 13) times—164 (184, 190, 204) sts.

Separate Sleeves: Knit to 1st m, remove m, slip 36 (40, 40, 44) sleeve sts to waste yarn, CO 2 sts, remove m, knit to next marker, remove m, slip 36 (40, 40, 44) sleeve sts to waste yarn, CO 2 sts, remove m, knit to end of rnd—96 (108, 114, 120) sts.

Knit even until piece measures 10.5 (13.5, 14.5, 15.5) in / 26.5 (34.5, 37, 39.5) cm from underarm.

Set-up Rnd: K1, place gusset marker, k46 (52, 55, 58), place gusset marker, k2, place gusset marker, knit to 1 st before BOR, place gusset marker, k1.

Inc Rnd: Knit to gusset m, m1L, sm, knit to next gusset m, sm, m1R, knit to next gusset m, M1L, sm, knit to next gusset m, sm, M1R, knit to end.

Repeat last 2 rnds until there are 11 sts between each set of gusset markers.

Split Legs: Knit to last gm, slip next 11 sts to waste yarn, turn and purl back to the back gusset sts, slip next 11 sts to waste yarn. Continue working left leg only in St st flat, until leg measures 2 (2.5, 2.75, 3) in / 5 (6.5, 7, 7.5) cm from split.

Note: If preferred here, you can place the right leg sts on waste yarn or a holder, but you can easily leave them on the other portion of the circular needle while working the left leg flat.

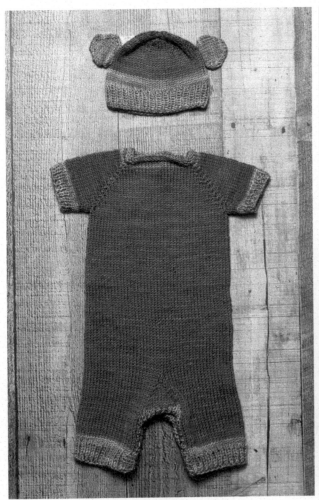

FRONT   **BACK**

Change to smaller needles and CC, and work K1, P1 Rib for 1 in / 2.5 cm. Bind off in Rib pattern. Repeat for second leg.

Gusset Snap Band

With smaller needles and CC and the RS of the romper front facing, start at the bottom right corner, and pick up and knit 2 sts for every 3 rows along the leg, move the 11 held sts onto spare needles and knit across, pick up and knit 2 sts for every 3 rows down left side. Knit every row for 1.5 in / 4 cm. Bind off all sts knitwise. Repeat for back side.

Sleeves

Move 36 (40, 40, 44) sleeve sts to dpn(s). Knit around sleeve sts, pick up and knit 2 sts, pm, pick up and knit 2 sts.

Knit 3 rnds.

Dec Rnd: K1, k2tog, knit to last 3 sts before m, ssk, k1—2 sts dec.

Even Rnd: Knit.

Rep Dec Rnd 1 (1, 0, 1) time more—36 (40, 42, 44) sts.

Switch to smaller needles and CC and work in K1, P1 Rib in the round for 3 rnds. Bind off in Rib pattern.

FINISHING

Sew buttons carefully on button band on opposite side matching buttonholes.

Using a sewing machine, or needle and thread, carefully sew snap tape along the RS of the gusset snap band.

Weave in all ends. Wash and block to measurements.

Hat

Using CC, CO 64 (72, 80, 88) sts. Place marker and join to work in the round, being careful not to twist your sts.

Work K1, P1 Rib for 1 in / 2.5 cm.

Knit 5 rnds.

Switch to MC and knit until hat measures 3.5 (3.5, 4, 5) in / 9 (9, 10, 12.5) cm from cast-on edge.

Dec Rnd: *K6, k2tog; repeat from * to end of rnd—56 (63, 70, 77) sts.

Knit 1 rnd.

Dec Rnd: *K5, k2tog; repeat from * to end of rnd—48 (54, 60, 66) sts.

Knit 2 rnds.

Dec Rnd: *K4, k2tog; repeat from * to end of rnd—40 (45, 50, 55) sts.

Knit 1 rnd.

Dec Rnd: *K3, k2tog; repeat from * to end of rnd—32 (36, 40, 44) sts.

Dec Rnd: *K2, k2tog; repeat from * to end of rnd—24 (27, 30, 33) sts.

Dec Rnd: K0 (1, 0, 1) *k2tog, repeat from * to end of rnd—12 (14, 15, 17) sts.

Dec Rnd: K0 (0, 1, 1), *k2tog, repeat from * to end of rnd—6 (7, 8, 9) sts.

Cut yarn leaving a 12 in / 30.5 cm tail. Weave tail through all remaining sts and pull tight to close.

Ears (make 2)

Fold hat in half, with CC, pick up 8 sts along side, 1.5 in / 4 cm from CO edge.

Pick up 8 sts directly across from those 8 sts—16 sts.

Knit 2 rnds.

Inc Rnd: *K1f&b, k6, k1f&b; rep form * once—20 sts.

Knit 1 rnd.

Inc Rnd: *K1f&b, k8, k1f&b; rep from * once—24 sts.

Knit 1 rnd.

Inc Rnd: *K1f&b, k10, k1f&b; rep from * once—28 sts.

Knit 2 rnds.

Dec Rnd: *Ssk, k8, k2tog; rep from * once—24 sts.

Knit 1 rnd.

Dec Rnd: *Ssk, k6, k2tog; rep from * once—20 sts.

Knit 1 rnd.

Dec Rnd: *Ssk, k4, k2tog; rep from * once—16 sts.

Knit 1 rnd.

Dec Rnd: *Ssk, k2, k2tog; rep from * once—12 sts.

Knit 1 rnd.

Dec Rnd: *Ssk, k2tog; rep from * once—8 sts.

Cut yarn, leaving a 12 in / 30.5 cm tail.

Use Kitchener stitch to graft the ear closed.

LET'S *Imagine!*

Pumpkin

Seriously, what is cuter than a little pumpkin, right? Almost like you picked it right out of the patch! This one would be super fun to change out the colors on to make it fit your favorite fruits or vegetables or dress it up for the different seasons.

Sizes: Newborn (6 months, 12 months, 18 months)

Finished Chest Circumference: 16 (18, 20, 22) in / 40.5 (45.5, 51, 56) cm

Gauge: 20 sts and 28 rows = 4 in / 10 cm in St st on larger needles

Yarn: Kim Dyes Yarn, Brioche DK (#3 light weight; 100% superwash merino wool; 280 yd / 256 m per 3.5 oz / 100 g): 2 (2, 3, 3) skeins Boo! (MC) and 1 (1, 1, 1) skein Dill Chip (CC)

Needles: US 7 (4.5 mm) 16 in / 40 cm circular, or size needed to obtain gauge; US 5 (3.75 mm) 16 in / 40 cm circular and dpn(s), or needles two sizes smaller than size needed to obtain gauge

Notions: Tapestry needle, three ½ in / 1.5 cm JHB buttons, 1 in / 2.5 cm wide snap tape, sewing needle and thread, waste yarn

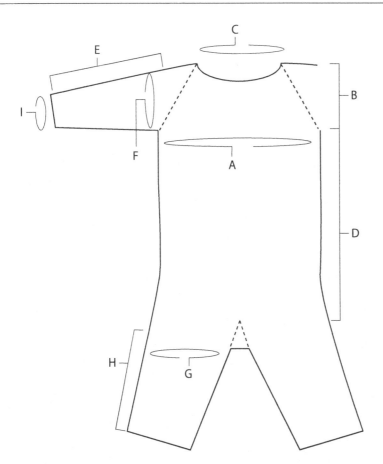

A - 16 (18, 20, 22) in
    40.5 (45.5, 51, 56) cm
B - 2.75 (3.5, 4, 4.5) in
    7 (9, 10, 11.5) cm
C - 9.75 (10.25, 11, 11.75) in
    25 (26, 28, 30) cm
D - 10.5 (13.5, 14.5, 15.5) in
    26.5 (34.5, 37, 39.5) cm
E - 5.5 (6, 7, 8) in
    14 (15, 19, 20.5) cm
F - 6 (6.75, 7.75, 8.75) in
    15 (17, 19.5, 22) cm
G - 8.25 (9, 9.75, 10.75) in
    21 (23, 25, 27.5) cm
H - 6 (7, 9, 10) in
    15 (19, 23, 25.5) cm
I - 4.75 (5.5, 6.5, 7.5) in
    12 (14, 16.5, 19) cm

INSTRUCTIONS

Body

With MC, cast on CO 49 (51, 55, 59) sts.

Set-up Row 1 (RS): K5 sts (button band), pm, k6 (6, 7, 7) front sts, pm, k6 (6, 7, 8) sleeve sts, pm, k15 (17, 17, 19) back sts, pm, k6 (6, 7, 8) sleeve sts, pm, k6 (6, 7, 7) front sts, pm, k5 sts (button band).

Set-up Row 2 (WS): K5, purl to last 5 sts, k5 (slipping all markers as you come to them).

Inc Row (RS): K5, sm, (knit to 1 st before m, k1f&b sm, k1f&b) 4 times, knit to end of row—57 (59, 63, 67) sts.

Even Row (WS): K5, purl to last 5 sts, k5 (slipping all markers as you come to them).

Buttonhole Inc Row (RS): K2, yo, k2tog, k1, sm, (knit to 1st before m, k1f&b, sm, k1f&b) 4 times, knit to end of row—65 (67, 71, 75) sts.

Even Row (WS): K5, purl to last 5 sts, k5 (slipping all markers as you come to them).

Inc Row (RS): K5, sm, (knit to 1 st before m, k1f&b sm, k1f&b) 4 times, knit to end of row—8 sts increased.

Repeat last two rows 2 (3, 4, 5) times more—89 (99, 111, 123) sts.

Then work one more WS Even Row.

Buttonhole Inc Row (RS): K2, yo, k2tog, k1, sm, (knit to 1st before m, k1f&b, sm, k1f&b) 4 times, knit to end of row—97 (107, 119, 131) sts.

Even Row (WS): K5, purl to last 5 sts, k5 (slipping all markers as you come to them).

Inc Row (RS): K5, sm, (knit to 1 st before m, k1f&b sm, k1f&b) 4 times, knit to end of row—8 sts increased.

Repeat last two rows 1 (2, 3, 4) times more—113 (131, 151, 171) sts.

Then work one more WS Even Row.

Buttonhole Inc Row (RS): K2, yo, k2tog, k1, sm, (knit to 1st before m, k1f&b, sm, k1f&b) 4 times, knit to end of row—121 (139, 159, 179) sts.

Even Row (WS): K5, purl to last 5 sts, k5 (slipping all markers as you come to them).

Joining Row (RS): K5, sm, (knit to 1 st before m, k1f&b sm, k1f&b) 4 times, knit to last 5 sts. Slip 5 sts purlwise from the LH needle to spare dpn, then k2tog using 1 st from the RH needle and 1 st from dpn five times—124 (142, 162, 182) sts.

Cut yarn, leaving a 12 in / 30.5 cm tail, slip 16 (18, 21, 23) sts purlwise to the RH needle (all the sts before the first sleeve m).

Separate Sleeves: Remove m, then move 26 (30, 35, 40) sleeve sts to waste yarn, CO 2 sts,

FRONT

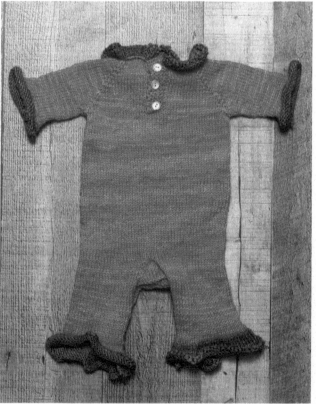

BACK

place new BOR m, CO 2 sts, remove m, knit to next m, remove m, move 26 (30, 35, 40) sleeve sts to waste yarn, CO 2 sts, pm, CO 2 sts, knit to end of rnd.

Knit every rnd until piece measures 10.5 (13.5, 14.5, 15.5) in / 26.5 (34.5, 37, 39.5) cm from underarm.

Gusset

Set-up Rnd 1: K19 (22, 24, 27) sts, place gusset m, k1, place gusset m, k39 (44, 49, 54) sts, place gusset m, k1, place gusset m, knit to end.

Set-up Rnd 2: Knit.

Gusset Inc Rnd: Knit to gusset m, sm, *m1L, knit to m, m1R, sm; rep from * once, knit to end.

Even Rnd: Knit.

Repeat last 2 rnds four times more, until there are 11 sts between the gusset markers.

Split Legs: Knit to last gusset m, slip next 11 sts to waste yarn, turn and purl back to the back gusset sts, slip next 11 sts to waste yarn. Continue working left leg only in St st flat, until leg measures 5 (6, 8, 9) in / 12.5 (15, 20.5, 23) cm from leg separation.

Bind off all sts knitwise.

Note: If preferred here, you can place the right leg sts on waste yarn or a holder, but you can easily leave them on the other portion of the circular needle while working the left leg flat.

Switch to CC, work k1, k1f&b around the entire leg.

Work in St st for 1 in / 2.5 cm.

Gusset Snap Band: With smaller needles and RS facing and starting at the bottom right corner of the front above the Rib stitch, pick up and knit 2 sts for every 3 sts along the leg, move the 11 held gusset sts on to spare needles and knit across, pick up and knit 2 sts for every 3 sts along the leg. Knit every row for 1.5 in / 4 cm. Bind off all sts. Repeat for back side.

Sleeves

Move 26 (30, 35, 40) sleeve sts to dpns.

Reattach yarn and knit around sleeve sts, pick up and knit 2 sts, pm, pick up and knit 2 sts—30 (34, 39, 44) sts.

Knit 3 rnds.

Dec Rnd: K1, k2tog, knit to last 3 sts before m, ssk, k1—28 (32, 37, 42) sts.

Knit 10 (10, 12, 14) rnds.

Dec Rnd: K1, k2tog, knit to last 3 sts before m,
   ssk, k1—26 (30, 35, 40) sts.
Knit 10 (10, 12, 14) rnds.
Dec Rnd: K1, k2tog, knit to last 3 sts before m,
   ssk, k1—24 (28, 33, 38) sts.
Knit until sleeve measures 4.5 (5, 6, 7) in / 11.5
   (12.5, 15, 18) cm from underarm.
Final Dec Rnd (Size 12 Month Only): K1, k2tog,
   knit to end—24 (28, 32, 38) sts.
Switch to CC, work k1, k1f&b around the
   entire sleeve.
Work in St st for 1 in / 2.5 cm.
Bind off all sts knitwise.

NECK EDGING
With CC and smaller needles, starting at the
   right front edge immediately following
   the button band, pick up and knit 34 (42,
   50, 56) sts.
Work k1, k1f&b around the entire neck edging.
Work in St st for 1 in / 2.5 cm.
Bind off all sts knitwise.

FINISHING

Sew buttons carefully on button band on
   opposite side matching buttonholes.
Using a sewing machine, or needle and thread,
   carefully sew snap tape along the RS of the
   gusset snap band.
Weave in all ends. Wash and block to
   measurements.

Dinosaur

My kids all love to pretend to be a T-Rex, screaming "ROAR!" all over the house and creating chaos. Have so much prehistoric fun with this one as your little one gets to play pretend and ROAR all day long in this dinosaur romper.

Sizes: Newborn (6 months, 12 months, 18 months)

Finished Chest Circumference: 16 (18, 19, 20) in / 40.5 (45.5, 48.5, 51) cm

Gauge: 20 sts and 28 rows = 4 in / 10 cm in St st on larger needles

Yarn: Destination Yarn, Souvenir, DK Weight (#3 light weight; 100% superwash merino wool; 231 yd / 211 m per 3.5 oz / 100 g): 2 (2, 3, 3, 3) skeins Spice (MC) and 1 skein Shining Sea (CC)

Needles: US 5 (3.75 mm) 16 in / 40 cm circular, or size needed to obtain gauge; US 4 (3.5 mm) 16 in / 40 cm circular and dpn(s), or needles one size smaller than size needed to obtain gauge

Notions: Tapestry needle, three ½ in / 1.5 cm JHB buttons, 1 in / 2.5 cm wide snap tape, sewing machine or sewing needle and thread, waste yarn

Stitch Guide

K1, P1 RIB WORKED FLAT

Row 1: *K1, p1; rep from * to end of row.
Row 2: *P1, k1; rep from * to end of row.
Repeat Rows 1 and 2 for pattern.

K1, P1 RIB IN THE ROUND

Rnd 1: *K1, p1; rep from * to end of rnd.
Repeat Rnd 1 for pattern.

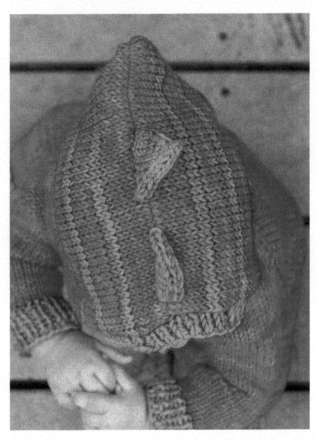

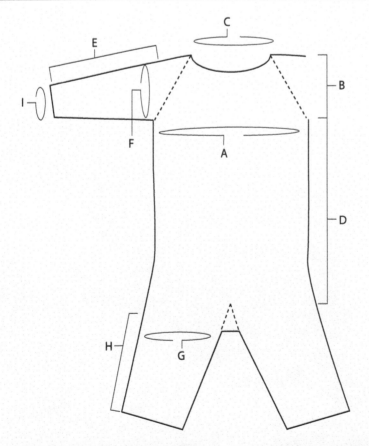

A - 16 (18, 19, 20) in
40.5 (45.5, 48.5, 51) cm
B - 3.25 (3.75, 4, 4.25) in
8.5 (9.5, 10, 11) cm
C - 9.5 (10.25, 10.75, 11.5) in
24 (26, 27.5, 29) cm
D - 10.5 (13.5, 14.5, 15.5) in
26.5 (34.5, 37, 39.5) cm
E - 7.5 (8.25, 9, 10) in
19 (21, 23, 25.5) cm
F - 6.25 (7.25, 7.75, 8.5) in
16 (18.5, 19.5, 21.5) cm
G - 8.25 (9, 9.5, 9.75) in
21 (23, 24, 25) cm
H - 5.5 (6.5, 7.5, 8.5) in
14 (16.5, 19, 21.5) cm
I - 5 (6, 6.5, 7.25) in
12.5 (15, 16.5, 18.5) cm

INSTRUCTIONS

Body

With larger needles, CO 47 (51, 54, 57) sts.

Set-up Row 1 (RS): K5 sts (button band), pm, k6 front sts, pm, k5 (6, 7, 8) sleeve sts, pm, 15 (17, 18, 19) back sts, pm, k5 (6, 7, 8) sleeve sts, pm, k6 front sts, pm, k5 sts (button band).

Set-up Row 2 (WS): K5, purl to last 5 sts, k5 (slipping all markers as you come to them).

Inc Row (RS): K5, sm, (knit to 1 st before m, k1f&b sm, k1f&b) 4 times, knit to end of row—55 (59, 62, 65) sts.

Even Row (WS): K5, purl to last 5 sts, k5 (slipping all markers as you come to them).

Buttonhole Inc Row (RS): K2, yo, k2tog, k1, sm, (knit to 1st before m, k1f&b, sm, k1f&b) 4 times, knit to end of row—63 (67, 70, 73) sts.

Even Row (WS): K5, purl to last 5 sts, k5 (slipping all markers as you come to them).

Inc Row (RS): K5, sm, (knit to 1 st before m, k1f&b sm, k1f&b) 4 times, knit to end of row—8 sts increased.

Repeat last two rows 2 (3, 4, 4) times more—87 (99, 110, 113) sts.

Then work one more WS Even Row.

Buttonhole Inc Row (RS): K2, yo, k2tog, k1, sm, (knit to 1st before m, k1f&b, sm, k1f&b) 4 times, knit to end of row—95 (107, 118, 121) sts.

Even Row (WS): K5, purl to last 5 sts, k5 (slipping all markers as you come to them).

Inc Row (RS): K5, sm, (knit to 1 st before m, k1f&b sm, k1f&b) 4 times, knit to end of row—8 sts increased.

Repeat last two rows 2 (3, 3, 4) times more—119 (139, 150, 161) sts.

Then work one more WS Even Row.

Buttonhole Inc Row (RS): K2, yo, k2tog, k1, sm, (knit to 1st before m, k1f&b, sm, k1f&b) 4 times, knit to end of row—127 (147, 158, 169) sts.

Even Row (WS): K5, purl to last 5 sts, k5 (slipping all markers as you come to them).

Joining Row (RS): K5, sm, (knit to 1 st before m, k1f&b sm, k1f&b) 4 times, knit to last 5 sts. Slip 5 sts purlwise from the LH needle to spare dpn, then k2tog using 1 st from the RH needle and 1 st from dpn five times—130 (150, 161, 172) sts.

Separate Sleeves: Remove m, knit to next m, then move 27 (32, 35, 38) sleeve sts to waste yarn, CO 1 st, place new BOR m, CO 1 st, remove m, knit to next m, remove m, move 27

FRONT

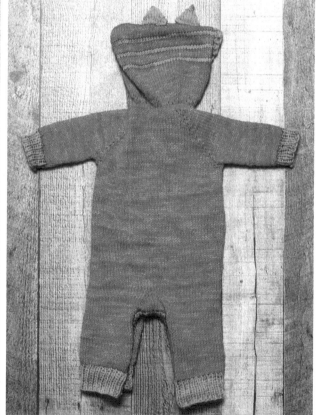

BACK

(32, 35, 38) sleeve sts to waste yarn, CO 1 st, pm, CO 1 st, knit to end of rnd.

Knit every rnd until piece measures 10.5 (13.5, 14.5, 15.5) in / 26.5 (34.5, 37, 39.5) cm from underarm.

Gusset

Set-up Rnd 1: K19 (22, 23, 25) sts, place gusset m, k1, place gusset m, k40 (45, 48, 50) sts, place gusset m, k1, place gusset m, knit to end.

Set-up Rnd 2: Knit.

Gusset Inc Rnd: Knit to gusset m, sm, *m1L, knit to m, m1R, sm; rep from * once, knit to end.

Even Rnd: Knit.

Repeat last 2 rnds four times more, until there are 11 sts between the gusset markers.

Split Legs: Knit to last gusset m, slip next 11 sts to waste yarn, turn and purl back to the back gusset sts, slip next 11 sts to waste yarn. Continue working left leg only in St st flat, until leg measures 4 (5, 6, 7) in / 10 (12.5, 15, 18) cm from split.

Note: If preferred here, you can place the right leg sts on waste yarn or a holder, but you can easily leave them on the other portion of the circular needle while working the left leg flat.

Switch to smaller needles and CC and work one row.

Work in K1, P1 Rib for 1.5 in / 4 cm.

Gusset Snap Band: With smaller needles and RS facing and starting at the bottom right corner of the front above the Rib stitch, pick up and knit 2 sts for every 3 sts along the leg, move the 11 held gusset sts on to spare needles and knit across, pick up and knit 2 sts for every 3 sts along the leg. Knit every row for 1.5 in / 4 cm. Bind off all sts. Repeat for back side.

Sleeves

Move 27 (32, 35, 38) sleeve sts to dpns. Reattach yarn and knit around sleeve sts, pick up and knit 2 sts, pm, pick up and knit 2 sts—31 (36, 39, 42) sts.

Knit 3 rnds.

Dec Rnd: K1, k2tog, knit to last 3 sts before m, ssk, k1—29 (34, 37, 40) sts.

Knit 10 (10, 12, 14) rnds.

Dec Rnd: K1, k2tog, knit to last 3 sts before m, ssk, k1—27 (32, 35, 38) sts.

Knit 10 (10, 12, 14) rnds.

Dec Rnd: K1, k2tog, knit to last 3 sts before m, ssk, k1—25 (30, 33, 36) sts.

Knit until sleeve measures 5.5 (6.25, 7, 8) in / 14 (16, 17, 20.5) cm from underarm.

Final Dec Rnd (Sizes Newborn & 12 Month Only): K1, k2tog, knit to end—24 (30, 32, 36) sts.

Switch to smaller needles and CC, work in K1, P1 Rib for 2 in / 5 cm. Bind off all sts in Rib pattern.

Hood

Begin at right front edge with larger needles, pick up and knit 36 (40, 40, 44) sts.
Next Row (WS): Purl.
Inc Row 1 (RS): *K1, k1f&b; rep from * to end— 54 (60, 60, 66) sts.
Next Row: Purl.
Inc Row 2: *K2, k1f&b; rep from * to end of row—72 (80, 80, 88) sts.
Work in St st until hood measures 3 in / 7.5 cm.
Switch to CC and work 2 rows.
Switch back to MC and work 4 rows.
Continue in this stripe pattern until hood measures 7 (7, 7.5, 8) in / 18 (18, 19, 20.5) cm.
Using Kitchener stitch, graft hood closed using same color as final stripe.

HOOD EDGING

With CC and smaller needles and beginning at right front edge after the button band, pick up and knit 2 sts for every 3 sts around the front, the hood, and the left front.
Work in K1, P1 Rib for 3 rows. Bind off in Rib pattern.

Spikes (make 2)

Using dpn(s) and CC, CO 20 sts, pm, and join to work in the rnd.
Rnds 1 and 2: Knit.
Rnd 3: *Ssk, k6, k2tog; rep from * once—16 sts.
Rnd 4: Knit.
Rnd 5: *Ssk, k4, k2tog; rep from * once—12 sts.
Rnd 6: Knit.
Rnd 7: *Ssk, k2, k2tog; rep from * once—8 sts.
Rnd 8: Knit.
Rnd 9: *Ssk, k2tog; rep from * once—4 sts.
Rnd 10: *K2tog; rep from * once—2 sts.
Cut yarn and pull tight through remaining 2 sts.
Sew spikes to the top of the hood, using photos as a guide.

FINISHING

Using a sewing machine, or needle and thread, sew snap tape on the gusset button band.
Sew buttons opposite buttonholes.
Weave in all ends. Wash and block.

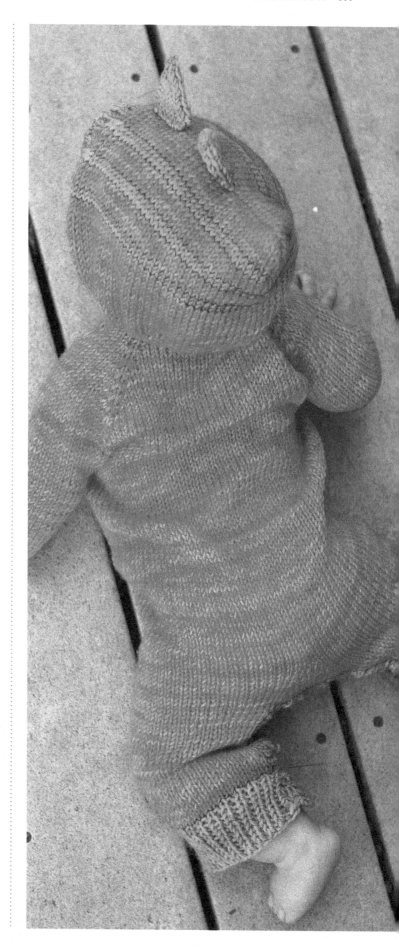

FRIENDLY NEIGHBORHOOD
Tiger or Honey Bear

My littlest one loves cuddling up and watching *Mister Rogers' Neighborhood*, which makes my heart literally sing for joy because I have such fond memories of Mister Rogers myself. My favorite puppet has always been a certain shy tiger, and I was so happy when he got his own cartoon show a few years ago. It quickly became a household favorite, and I couldn't leave him out. If you love a certain honey bear, this pattern also works for him!

Sizes: Newborn (6 months, 12 months, 18 months)

Finished Chest Circumference: 16 (18, 19, 20) in/ 40.5 (45.5, 48.5, 51) cm

Gauge: 20 sts and 28 rows = 4 in / 10 cm in St st on larger needles

Yarn: SweetGeorgia Yarns, Superwash DK (#3 light weight; 100% superwash merino; 256 yd / 234 m per 4 oz / 115 g): 2 (2, 3, 3) skeins Lemon Curd (MC) and 1 (1, 1, 1) skein Cherry (CC)

Needles: US 5 (3.75 mm) 16 in / 40 cm circular, or size needed to obtain gauge; US 4 (3.5 mm) 16 in / 40 cm circular and dpn(s), or needles one size smaller than size needed to obtain gauge

Notions: Tapestry needle, three ½ in / 1.5 cm JHB buttons, 1 in / 2.5 cm wide snap tape, sewing machine or sewing needle and thread, waste yarn

Stitch Guide

K1, P1 RIB WORKED FLAT

Row 1: *K1, p1; rep from * to end of row.
Row 2: *P1, k1; rep from * to end of row.
Repeat Rows 1 and 2 for pattern.

K1, P1 RIB IN THE ROUND

Rnd 1: *K1, p1; rep from * to end of rnd.
Repeat Rnd 1 for pattern.

INSTRUCTIONS

Body

With larger needles and CC, CO 47 (51, 54, 57) sts.

Set-up Row 1 (RS): K5 sts (button band), pm, k6 front sts, pm, k5 (6, 7, 8) sleeve sts, pm, 15 (17, 18, 19) back sts, pm, k5 (6, 7, 8) sleeve sts, pm, k6 front sts, pm, k5 sts (button band).

Set-up Row 2 (WS): K5, purl to last 5 sts, k5 (slipping all markers as you come to them).

Inc Row (RS): K5, sm, (knit to 1 st before m, k1f&b sm, k1f&b) 4 times, knit to end of row— 55 (59, 62, 65) sts.

Even Row (WS): K5, purl to last 5 sts, k5 (slipping all markers as you come to them).

Buttonhole Inc Row (RS): K2, yo, k2tog, k1, sm, (knit to 1st before m, k1f&b, sm, k1f&b) 4 times, knit to end of row—63 (67, 70, 73) sts.

Even Row (WS): K5, purl to last 5 sts, k5 (slipping all markers as you come to them).

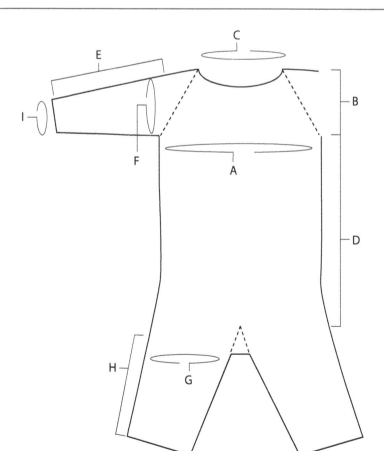

A - 16 (18, 19, 20) in
   40.5 (45.5, 48.5, 51) cm
B - 3.25 (3.75, 4, 4.25) in
   8.5 (9.5, 10, 11) cm
C - 9.5 (10.25, 10.75, 11.5) in
   24 (26, 27.5, 29) cm
D - 10.5 (13.5, 14.5, 15.5) in
   26.5 (34.5, 37, 39.5) cm
E - 7.5 (8.25, 9, 10) in
   19 (21, 23, 25.5) cm
F - 6.25 (7.25, 7.75, 8.5) in
   16 (18.5, 19.5, 21.5) cm
G - 8.25 (9, 9.5, 9.75) in
   21 (23, 24, 25) cm
H - 5.5 (6.5, 7.5, 8.5) in
   14 (16.5, 19, 21.5) cm
I - 5 (6, 6.5, 7.25) in
   12.5 (15, 16.5, 18.5) cm

Inc Row (RS): K5, sm, (knit to 1 st before m, k1f&b sm, k1f&b) 4 times, knit to end of row—8 sts increased.

Repeat last two rows 2 (3, 4, 4) times more—87 (99, 110, 113) sts.

Then work one more WS Even Row.

Buttonhole Inc Row (RS): K2, yo, k2tog, k1, sm, (knit to 1st before m, k1f&b, sm, k1f&b) 4 times, knit to end of row—95 (107, 118, 121) sts.

Even Row (WS): K5, purl to last 5 sts, k5 (slipping all markers as you come to them).

Inc Row (RS): K5, sm, (knit to 1 st before m, k1f&b sm, k1f&b) 4 times, knit to end of row—8 sts increased.

Repeat last two rows 2 (3, 3, 4) times more—119 (139, 150, 161) sts.

Then work one more WS Even Row.

Buttonhole Inc Row (RS): K2, yo, k2tog, k1, sm, (knit to 1st before m, k1f&b, sm, k1f&b) 4 times, knit to end of row—127 (147, 158, 169) sts.

Even Row (WS): K5, purl to last 5 sts, k5 (slipping all markers as you come to them).

Joining Row (RS): K5, sm, (knit to 1 st before m, k1f&b sm, k1f&b) 4 times, knit to last 5 sts. Slip 5 sts purlwise from the LH needle to spare dpn, then k2tog using 1 st from the RH

needle and 1 st from dpn five times—130 (150, 161, 172) sts.

Separate Sleeves: Remove m, knit to next m, then move 27 (32, 35, 38) sleeve sts to waste yarn, CO 1 st, place new BOR m, CO 1 st, remove m, knit to next m, remove m, move 27 (32, 35, 38) sleeve sts to waste yarn, CO 1 st, pm, CO 1 st, knit to end of rnd.

Knit for 2 in / 5 cm.

Switch to MC and knit every rnd until piece measures 10.5 (13.5, 14.5, 15.5) in / 26.5 (34.5, 37, 39.5) cm from underarm.

Gusset

Set-up Rnd 1: K19 (22, 23, 25) sts, place gusset m, k1, place gusset m, k40 (45, 48, 50) sts, place gusset m, k1, place gusset m, knit to end.

Set-up Rnd 2: Knit.

Gusset Inc Rnd: Knit to gusset m, sm, *m1L, knit to m, m1R, sm; rep from * once, knit to end.

Even Rnd: Knit.

Repeat last 2 rnds four times more, until there are 11 sts between the gusset markers.

Split Legs: Knit to last gusset m, slip next 11 sts to waste yarn, turn and purl back to the back gusset sts, slip next 11 sts to waste yarn.

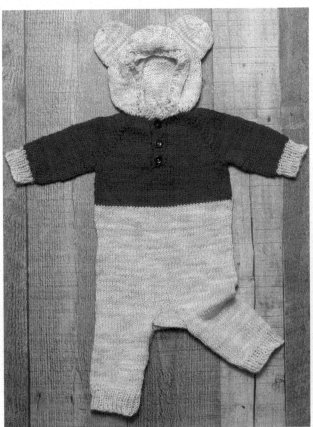

FRONT

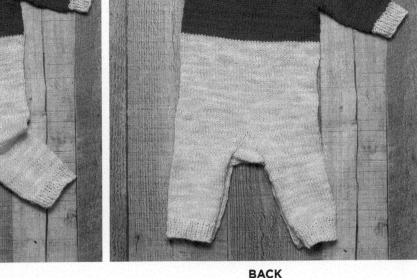

BACK

Continue working left leg only in St st flat, until leg measures 4 (5, 6, 7) in / 10 (12.5, 15, 18) cm from split.

Note: If preferred here, you can place the right leg sts on waste yarn or a holder, but you can easily leave them on the other portion of the circular needle while working the left leg flat.

Switch to smaller needles and work in K1, P1 Rib for 1.5 in / 4 cm.

Gusset Snap Band: With smaller needles and RS facing and starting at the bottom right corner of the front above the Rib stitch, pick up and knit 2 sts for every 3 sts along the leg, move the 11 held gusset sts on to spare needles and knit across, pick up and knit 2 sts for every 3 sts along the leg. Knit every row for 1.5 in / 4 cm. Bind off all sts knitwise. Repeat for back side.

Sleeves

Move 27 (32, 35, 38) sleeve sts to dpns.

Reattach CC and knit around sleeve sts, pick up and knit 2 sts, pm, pick up and knit 2 sts—31 (36, 39, 42) sts.

Knit 3 rnds.

Dec Rnd: K1, k2tog, knit to last 3 sts before m, ssk, k1—29 (34, 37, 40) sts.

Knit 10 (10, 12, 14) rnds.

Dec Rnd: K1, k2tog, knit to last 3 sts before m, ssk, k1—27 (32, 35, 38) sts.

Knit 10 (10, 12, 14) rnds.

Dec Rnd: K1, k2tog, knit to last 3 sts before m, ssk, k1—25 (30, 33, 36) sts.

Knit until sleeve measures 5.5 (6.25, 7, 8) in / 14 (16, 17, 20.5) cm from underarm.

Final Dec Rnd (Sizes Newborn & 12 Month Only): K1, k2tog, knit to end—24 (30, 32, 36) sts.

Switch to smaller needles and MC and work in K1, P1 Rib for 2 in / 5 cm. Bind off all sts in Rib pattern.

Hood

Begin at right front edge with larger needles and MC, pick up and knit 36 (40, 40, 44) sts.

Next Row (WS): Purl.

Inc Row 1 (RS): *K1, k1f&b; rep from * to end—54 (60, 60, 66) sts.

Next Row: Purl.

Inc Row 2: K0 (0, 0, 2), *k2, k1f&b; rep from * to end of row—72 (80, 80, 88) sts.

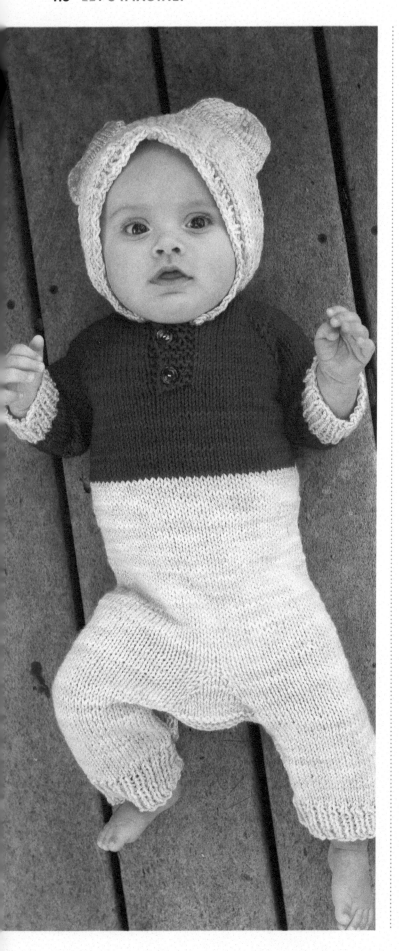

Work in St st until hood measures 7 (7, 7.5, 8) in / 18 (18, 19, 20.5) cm.
Using Kitchener stitch, graft hood closed.

HOOD EDGING

With smaller needles and beginning at right front edge after the button band, pick up and knit 2 sts for every 3 sts around the front, the hood and the left front.
Work in K1, P1 Rib for 3 rows. Bind off all sts in Rib pattern.

Ears (Make 2)

With dpn(s) and MC, CO 32 sts, dividing evenly between 2 needles.
Knit for 8 rnds.
Dec Rnd: *K6, k2tog; rep from * to end of rnd—28 sts.
Knit 2 rnds.
Dec Rnd: *K5, k2tog; rep from * to end of rnd—24 sts.
Knit 1 rnd.
Dec Rnd: *K4, k2tog; rep from * to end of rnd—20 sts.
Knit 1 rnd.
Cut yarn and pull tight through remaining sts.
Sew ears to either side of hood, using photos as a guide.

FINISHING

Using a sewing machine, or needle and thread, sew snap tape on the gusset button band.
Sew buttons opposite buttonholes.
Weave in all ends. Wash and block.

Unicorn

Because unicorns are real! What's more fun than dressing up a baby as a unicorn? Think of all the different color variations you can put together for this one. The magic is in finding a set of mini skeins that really make your unicorn heart sing!

Sizes: Newborn (6 months, 12 months, 18 months)

Finished Chest Circumference: 16 (18, 19, 20) in / 40.5 (45.5, 48.5, 51) cm

Gauge: 20 sts and 28 rows = 4 in / 10 cm in St st on larger needles

Yarn: SweetGeorgia Yarns, Superwash DK (#3 light weight; 100% superwash merino; 256 yd / 234 m per 4 oz / 115 g): 2 (2, 3, 3) skeins Lilac (MC) and 1 set of Party of Five, Salt Water Taffy

Needles: US 5 (3.75 mm) 16 in / 40 cm circular, or size needed to obtain gauge; US 4 (3.5 mm) 16 in /40 cm circular and dpn(s), or needles one size smaller than size needed to obtain gauge

Notions: Tapestry needle, three ½ in / 1.5 cm JHB buttons, 1 in / 2.5 cm wide snap tape, sewing machine or sewing needle and thread, waste yarn

Stitch Guide

K1, P1 RIB WORKED FLAT

Row 1: *K1, p1; rep from * to end of row.
Row 2: *P1, k1; rep from * to end of row.
Repeat Rows 1 and 2 for pattern.

K1, P1 RIB IN THE ROUND

Rnd 1: *K1, p1; rep from * to end of rnd.
Repeat Rnd 1 for pattern.

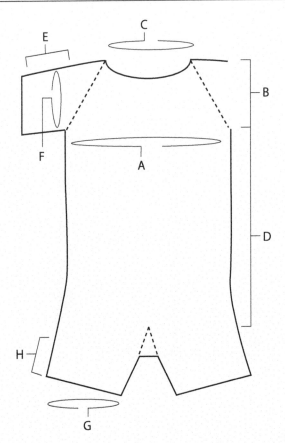

A - 16 (18, 19, 20) in
   40.5 (45.5, 48.5, 51) cm
B - 3.25 (3.5, 4, 4.25) in
   8.5 (9, 10, 11) cm
C - 9.5 (11, 11.75, 13.5) in
   24 (28, 30, 34.5) cm
D - 10.5 (13.5, 14.5, 15.5) in
   26.5 (34.5, 37, 39.5) cm
E - 2.5 in / 5 cm
F - 6 (6.5, 7.5, 8.25) in
   15 (16.5, 19, 21) cm
G - 9.5 (10.5, 11.5, 12.5) in
   24 (26.5, 29, 32) cm
H - 4.5 (4.5, 5.5, 5.5) in
   11.5 (11.5, 14, 14) cm

INSTRUCTIONS

Body

With larger needles, CO 47 (51, 54, 57) sts.

Set-up Row 1 (RS): K5 sts (button band), pm, k6 front sts, pm, k5 (6, 7, 8) sleeve sts, pm, 15 (17, 18, 19) back sts, pm, k5 (6, 7, 8) sleeve sts, pm, k6 front sts, pm, k5 sts (button band).

Set-up Row 2 (WS): K5, purl to last 5 sts, k5 (slipping all markers as you come to them).

Inc Row (RS): K5, sm, (knit to 1 st before m, k1f&b sm, k1f&b) 4 times, knit to end of row—55 (59, 62, 65) sts.

Even Row (WS): K5, purl to last 5 sts, k5 (slipping all markers as you come to them).

Buttonhole Inc Row (RS): K2, yo, k2tog, k1, sm, (knit to 1st before m, k1f&b, sm, k1f&b) 4 times, knit to end of row—63 (67, 70, 73) sts.

Even Row (WS): K5, purl to last 5 sts, k5 (slipping all markers as you come to them).

Inc Row (RS): K5, sm, (knit to 1 st before m, k1f&b sm, k1f&b) 4 times, knit to end of row—8 sts increased.

Repeat last two rows 2 (3, 4, 4) times more—87 (99, 110, 113) sts.

Then work one more WS Even Row.

Buttonhole Inc Row (RS): K2, yo, k2tog, k1, sm, (knit to 1st before m, k1f&b, sm, k1f&b) 4 times, knit to end of row—95 (107, 118, 121) sts.

Even Row (WS): K5, purl to last 5 sts, k5 (slipping all markers as you come to them).

Inc Row (RS): K5, sm, (knit to 1 st before m, k1f&b sm, k1f&b) 4 times, knit to end of row—8 sts increased.

Repeat last two rows 2 (3, 3, 4) times more—119 (139, 150, 161) sts.

Then work one more WS Even Row.

Buttonhole Inc Row (RS): K2, yo, k2tog, k1, sm, (knit to 1st before m, k1f&b, sm, k1f&b) 4 times, knit to end of row—127 (147, 158, 169) sts.

Even Row (WS): K5, purl to last 5 sts, k5 (slipping all markers as you come to them).

Joining Row (RS): K5, sm, (knit to 1 st before m, k1f&b sm, k1f&b) 4 times, knit to last 5 sts. Slip 5 sts purlwise from LH needle to spare dpn, then k2tog using 1 st from RH needle and 1 st from dpn five times—130 (150, 161, 172) sts.

FRONT

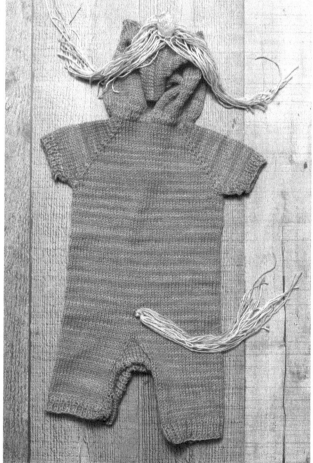

BACK

Separate Sleeves: Remove m, knit to next m, then move 27 (32, 35, 38) sleeve sts to waste yarn, CO 1 st, place new BOR m, CO 1 st, remove m, knit to next m, remove m, move 27 (32, 35, 38) sleeve sts to waste yarn, CO 1 st, pm, CO 1 st, knit to end of rnd.

Knit every rnd until piece measures 10.5 (13.5, 14.5, 15.5) in / 26.5 (34.5, 37, 39.5) cm from underarm.

Gusset

Set-up Rnd 1: K19 (22, 23, 25) sts, place gusset m, k1, place gusset m, k40 (45, 48, 50) sts, place gusset m, k1, place gusset m, knit to end.

Set-up Rnd 2: Knit.

Gusset Inc Rnd: Knit to gusset m, sm, *m1L, knit to m, m1R, sm; rep from * once, knit to end.

Even Rnd: Knit.

Repeat last 2 rnds four times more, until there are 11 sts between the gusset markers.

Split Legs: Knit to last gusset m, slip next 11 sts to waste yarn, turn and purl back to back gusset sts, slip next 11 sts to waste yarn. Continue working left leg only in St st flat, until leg measures 3 (3, 4, 4) in / 7.5 (7.5, 10, 10) cm from split.

Note: If preferred here, you can place the right leg sts on waste yarn or a holder, but you can easily leave them on the other portion of the circular needle while working the left leg flat.

Switch to smaller needles and work in K1, P1 Rib for 1.5 in / 4 cm. Bind off all sts in Rib pattern.

Gusset Snap Band: With smaller needles and RS facing and starting at the bottom right corner of the front above the Rib stitch, pick up and knit 2 sts for every 3 sts along the leg, move the 11 held gusset sts on to spare needles and knit across, pick up and knit 2 sts for every 3 sts along the leg. Knit every row for 1.5 in / 4 cm. Bind off all sts knitwise. Repeat for back side.

Sleeves

Move 27 (32, 35, 38) sleeve sts to dpns.

Reattach yarn and knit around sleeve sts, pick up and knit 2 sts, pm, pick up and knit 2 sts—31 (36, 39, 42) sts.

Knit 3 rnds.

Switch to smaller needles and work in K1, P1 Rib for 2 in / 5 cm. Bind off all sts in Rib pattern.

Tail

Cut 5 strands of each Party of Five mini-skein, 24 in / 61 cm long. Using photos as a guide, thread each strand halfway through the back of the romper roughly 1.5 in / 4 cm above start of gusset and tie tightly to secure.

Hood

Begin at right front edge with larger needles, pick up and knit 36 (40, 40, 44) sts.
Next Row (WS): Purl.
Inc Row 1 (RS): *K1, k1f&b; rep from * to end—54 (60, 60, 66) sts.
Next Row: Purl.
Inc Row 2: K0 (0, 0, 2), *k2, k1f&b; rep from * to end of row—72 (80, 80, 88) sts.
Work in St st until hood measures 7 (7, 7.5, 8) in / 18 (18, 19, 20.5) cm.
Using Kitchener stitch, graft hood closed.

HOOD EDGING

With smaller needles and beginning at right front edge after the button band, pick up and knit 2 sts for every 3 sts around the front, the hood, and the left front.
Work in K1, P1 Rib for 3 rows. Bind off all sts in Rib pattern.

Ears (make 2)

Using dpn(s), CO 20 sts, pm and join to work in the rnd.
Rnds 1 and 2: Knit.
Rnd 3: *Ssk, k6, k2tog; rep from * once—16 sts.
Rnd 4: Knit.
Rnd 5: *Ssk, k4, k2tog; rep from * once—12 sts.
Rnd 6: Knit.
Rnd 7: *Ssk, k2, k2tog; rep from * once—8 sts.
Rnd 8: Knit.
Rnd 9: *Ssk, k2tog; rep from * once—4 sts.
Rnd 10: *K2tog; rep from * once—2 sts.
Cut yarn and pull tight through remaining 2 sts.
Sew ears to either side of hood, using photos as a guide.

Horn

With C1, CO 20 sts, join to work in the rnd.
Knit 6 rnds.
Dec Rnd: *K3, k2tog; rep from * to end of rnd—16 sts.
Knit 3 rnds.
Dec Rnd: *K2, k2tog; rep from * to end of rnd—12 sts.

Knit 1 rnd.
Dec Rnd: *K1, k2tog; rep from * to end of rnd—8 sts
Dec Rnd: *k2tog; rep from * to end of rnd—4 sts.
Dec Rnd: *k2tog; rep from * to end of rnd—2 sts.
K2tog, cut yarn and pull tight through last stitch.
Lightly stuff and sew to the top of the hood.

Mane

Cut 10 strands of each Party of Five mini-skein, 24 in / 61 cm long. Using photos as a guide, thread each strand halfway through and tie tightly to secure.

FINISHING

Using a sewing machine, or needle and thread, sew snap tape on the gusset button band.
Sew buttons opposite buttonholes.
Weave in all ends. Wash and block.

Alien

There's a certain little blue alien (Stitch, of course!) that has my heart! This romper is my special tribute to him, and of course who can resist a snuggly alien baby?

Sizes: Newborn (6 months, 12 months, 18 months)

Finished Chest Circumference: 16 (18, 20, 22) in / 40.5 (45.5, 51, 56) cm

Finished Head Circumference: 10.5 (12, 13.25, 14.5) in / 26.5 (30.5, 33.5, 37) cm

Gauge: 24 sts and 32 rows = 4 in / 10 cm in St st on larger needles

Yarn: Malabrigo Yarn, Arroyo DK (#3 light weight; 100% superwash merino; 335 yd / 306 m per 3.5 oz / 100 g): 2 (2, 3, 3) skeins Cian (MC) and 1 (1, 1, 1) skein Azul Profundo (CC)

Needles: US 6 (4.0 mm) 16 in / 40 cm circular, or size needed to obtain gauge; US 4 (3.5 mm) 16 in / 40 cm circular and dpn(s), or needles two sizes smaller than size needed to obtain gauge

Notions: Tapestry needle, three ½ in / 1.5 cm buttons, 1 in / 2.5 cm wide snap tape, sewing needle and thread, waste yarn

Stitch Guide

K1, P1 RIB WORKED FLAT

Row 1: *K1, p1; rep from * to end of row.
Row 2: *P1, k1; rep from * to end of row.
Repeat Rows 1 and 2 for Pattern.

K1, P1 IN THE ROUND

Rnd 1: *K1, p1; rep from * to end of rnd.
Repeat Rnd 1 for pattern.

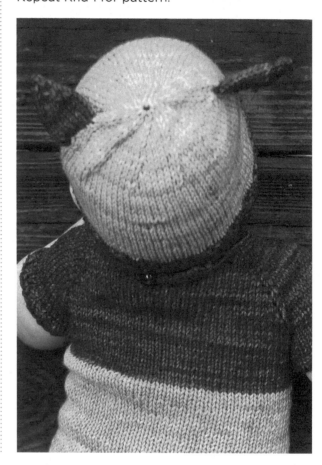

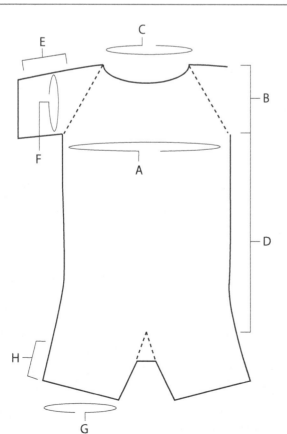

A - 16 (18, 20, 22) in
  40.5 (45.5, 51, 56) cm
B - 3.75 (4.25, 4.25, 4.5) in
  9.5 (11, 11, 11.5) cm
C - 7.75 (8.5, 9.5, 10.5) in
  19.5 (21.5, 24, 26.5) cm
D - 10.5 (13.5, 14.5, 15.5) in
  26.5 (34.5, 37, 39.5) cm
E - 1.5 (1.5, 1.25, 1.5) in
  4 (4, 3, 4) cm
F - 6 (6.75, 7, 7.25) in
  15 (17, 18, 18.5) cm
G - 9.25 (10.25, 10.75, 11.25) in
  23.5 (26, 27.5, 28.5) cm
H - 3 (3.5, 3.75, 4) in
  7.5 (9, 9.5, 10) cm

INSTRUCTIONS

Body

With CC and smaller needles, CO 47 (51, 57, 63) sts.

Set-up Row 1 (RS): K11 (11, 13, 13) front sts, pm, k6 (6, 6, 8) sleeve sts, pm, k16 (20, 22, 24) back sts, pm, k6 (6, 6, 8) sleeve sts, pm, k8 (8, 10, 10) front sts.

Set-up Row 2 (WS): Knit.

Set-up Row 3: Knit.

Buttonhole Row (WS): Knit to last 3 sts, k2tog, yo, k1.

Switch to larger needles and MC.

Inc Row (RS): (Knit to 1 st before m, k1f&b, sm, k1f&b) 4 times, knit to end—55 (59, 65, 71) sts.

Even Row (WS): K3, purl to last 3 sts, k3 (slipping all markers as you come to them).

Next Inc Row (RS): (Knit to 1 st before m, k1f&b, sm, k1f&b) 4 times, knit to end—63 (67, 73, 79) sts.

Buttonhole Row (WS): K3, purl to last 3 sts, k2tog, yo, k1.

Next Inc Row (RS): (Knit to 1 st before m, k1f&b, sm, k1f&b) 4 times, knit to end—71 (75, 81, 87) sts.

Row 8: K3, purl to last 3 sts, k3.

Joining Rnd (RS): Slip 3 sts purlwise from the RH needle to spare dpn, then k2tog using 1 st from the RH needle and 1 st from dpn three times. Join to work in the round and place a different type of marker to distinguish the start of the round, (knit to 1 st before m, k1f&b, sm, k1f&b) 4 times, knit to end of rnd—76 (80, 86, 92) sts.

Even Rnd: Knit.

Inc Rnd: (Knit to 1 st before m, k1f&b, sm, k1f&b) 4 times, knit to end—84 (88, 94, 100) sts.

Repeat last 2 rnds 10 (12, 12, 13) times—164 (184, 190, 204) sts.

Separate Sleeves:

Knit to 1st m, remove m, slip 36 (40, 40, 44) sleeve sts to waste yarn, CO 2 sts, remove m,

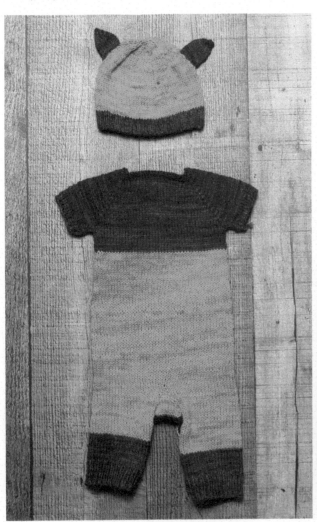

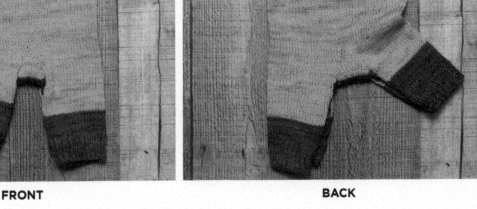

FRONT   **BACK**

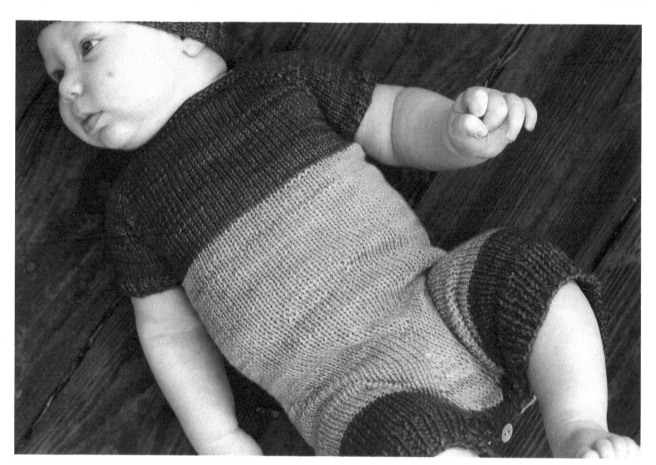

knit to next marker, remove m, slip 36 (40, 40, 44) sleeve sts to waste yarn, CO 2 sts, remove m, knit to end of rnd—96 (108, 114, 120) sts.

Knit even until piece measures 10.5 (13.5, 14.5, 15.5) in / 26.5 (34.5, 37, 39.5) cm from underarm.

Gusset

Set-up Rnd: K1, place gusset marker, k46 (52, 55, 58), place gusset marker, k2, place gusset marker, knit to 1 st before BOR, place gusset marker, k1.

Inc Rnd: Knit to gusset m, m1L, sm, knit to next gusset m, sm, m1R, knit to next gusset m, M1L, sm, knit to next gusset m, sm, M1R, knit to end.

Repeat last 2 rnds until there are 11 sts between each set of gusset markers.

Split Legs: Knit to last gm, slip next 11 sts to waste yarn, turn and purl back to the back gusset sts, slip next 11 sts to waste yarn. Continue working left leg only in St st flat, until leg measures 2 (2.5, 2.75, 3) in / 5 (6.5, 7, 7.5) cm from split.

Note: If preferred here, you can place the right leg sts on waste yarn or a holder, but you can

easily leave them on the other portion of the circular needle while working the left leg flat.

Change to smaller needles and CC, and work K1, P1 Rib for 1 in / 2.5 cm. Bind off all sts in Rib pattern.

Repeat for second leg.

Gusset Snap Band: With smaller needles and CC and the RS of the romper front facing, start at the bottom right corner, and pick up and knit 2 sts for every 3 rows along the leg, move the 11 held sts onto spare needles and knit across, pick up and knit 2 sts for every 3 rows down left side. Knit every row for 1.5 in / 4 cm. Bind off all sts knitwise. Repeat for back side.

Sleeves

Move 36 (40, 40, 44) sleeve sts to dpn(s). Knit around sleeve sts, pick up and knit 2 sts, pm, pick up and knit 2 sts.

Knit 3 rnds.

Dec Rnd: K1, k2tog, knit to last 3 sts before m, ssk, k1—2 sts decreased.

Even Rnd: Knit.

Rep Dec Rnd 1 (1, 0, 1) time more—36 (40, 42, 44) sts.

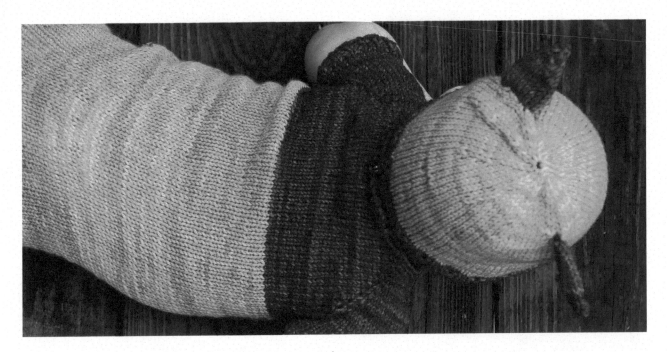

Switch to smaller needles and CC and work in K1, P1 Rib in the round for 3 rnds.
Bind off all sts in Rib pattern.

FINISHING

Sew buttons carefully on button band on opposite side matching buttonholes.
Using a sewing machine, or needle and thread, carefully sew snap tape along the RS of the gusset snap band.
Weave in all ends. Wash and block to measurements.

Hat

Using CC, CO 64 (72, 80, 88) sts. Place marker and join to work in the round, being careful not to twist your sts.
Work K1, P1 Rib for 1 in / 2.5 cm.
Knit 5 rnds.
Switch to MC and knit until hat measures 3.5 (3.5, 4, 5) in / 9 (9, 10, 12.5) cm from cast-on edge.
Dec Rnd: *K6, k2tog; repeat from * to end of rnd—56 (63, 70, 77) sts.
Knit 1 rnd.
Dec Rnd: *K5, k2tog; repeat from * to end of rnd—48 (54, 60, 66) sts.
Knit 2 rnds.
Dec Rnd: *K4, k2tog; repeat from * to end of rnd—40 (45, 50, 55) sts.
Knit 1 rnd.

Dec Rnd: *K3, k2tog; repeat from * to end of rnd—32 (36, 40, 44) sts.
Dec Rnd: *K2, k2tog; repeat from * to end of rnd. —24 (27, 30, 33) sts.
Dec Rnd: K0 (1, 0, 1) *k2tog, repeat from * to end of rnd—12 (14, 15, 17) sts.
Dec Rnd: K0 (0, 1, 1), *k2tog, repeat from * to end of rnd—6 (7, 8, 9) sts.
Cut yarn leaving a 12 in / 30.5 cm tail. Weave tail through all remaining sts and pull tight to close.

Antenna (make 2)

With CC, CO 16 sts, pm and join to knit in the rnd.
Knit 5 rnds.
Dec Rnd: *K2, k2tog; rep form * to end of rnd—12 sts.
Knit 1 rnd.
Dec Rnd: *K1, k2tog; rep from * to end of rnd—8 sts.
Dec Rnd: *K2tog; rep form * to end of rnd—4 sts.
Dec Rnd: *K2tog, rep from * to end of rnd—2 sts.
Cut yarn and pull tight through remaining 2 sts.
Sew antenna to the top of each side of the hat, using photos as a guide.

FINISHING

Weave in all ends. Wash and block to measurements.

Ballerina

Once a ballerina, always a ballerina. I spent many years of my childhood with dreams of Sugar Plum Fairies dancing in my head, not to mention the years I literally spent dancing through life. No matter whether your little one is graceful or not, this little ballerina set is sure to bring back memories, whether of your own ballet classes or special trips to the ballet.

Sizes: Newborn (3 months, 6 months, 9 months, 12 months, 18 months)

Finished Chest Circumference: 15 (16, 17, 18, 19, 20) in / 38 (40.5, 43, 45.5, 48.5, 51) cm

Gauge: 20 sts and 28 rows = 4 in / 10 cm in St st on larger needles

Yarn: SweetGeorgia Yarns, Superwash Worsted (#4 medium weight; 100% superwash merino wool; 200 yd / 182 m per 4 oz / 115 g): 2 (2, 2, 2, 2, 3) skeins Peony (MC)

SweetGeorgia Yarns, CashLuxe Spark (#1 super fine weight; 80% superwash merino wool, 10% cashmere, 10% silver-toned Stellina; 400 yd / 365 m per 4 oz / 115 g): 1 (1, 1, 1, 1, 1) skein Lady Grey (CC)

Needles: US 6 (4.0 mm) 16 in / 40 cm circular, or size needed to obtain gauge

Notions: Tapestry needle, 1 in / 2. 5 cm wide snap tape, sewing needle and thread

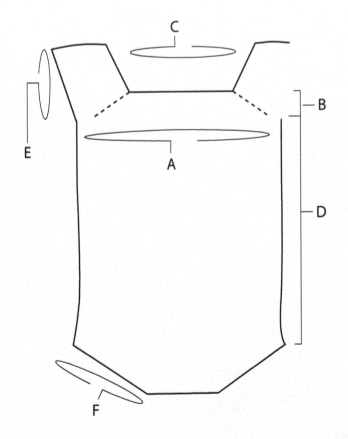

A - 15 (16, 17, 18, 19, 20) in
38 (40.5, 43, 45.5, 48.5, 51) cm

B - 1.5 (1.5, 1.75, 1.75, 2, 2) in
4 (4, 4.5, 4.5, 5, 5) cm

C - 13 (13.25, 14.5, 15.5, 15.75, 16.75) in
33 (33.5, 37, 39.5, 40, 42.5) cm

D - 6 (6.5, 7, 8, 8.5, 9) in
15 (16.5, 18, 20.5, 21.5, 23) cm

E - 5.25 (5.25, 6, 6.5, 6.75, 7.25) in
13.5 (13.5, 15, 16.5, 17, 18.5) cm

F - 7.5 (7.25, 8, 8.25, 9.25, 9) in
19 (18.5, 20.5, 21, 23.5, 23) cm

INSTRUCTIONS

Body

With MC, CO 65 (66, 73, 78, 79, 84) sts, pm, and join to work in the rnd, being careful not to twist your sts.

Set-up Rnd: K16 (16, 18, 20, 20, 22) sleeve sts, pm, k17 (17, 19, 19, 20, 20) back sts, pm, k16 (16, 18, 20, 20, 22) sleeve sts, pm, k16 (17, 18, 19, 19, 20) front sts.

Next Rnd: Knit.

Inc Rnd: (K1f&b, knit to 1 st before m, k1f&b, sm) 4 times—8 sts increased.

Even Rnd: Knit.

Repeat last two rnds 4 (4, 5, 5, 6, 6) times more—105 (106, 121, 126, 135, 140) sts.

Next Rnd (Create Shoulders): Remove m, bind off 26 (26, 30, 32, 34, 36) sleeve sts, remove m, knit across 27 (27, 31, 31, 34, 34) back sts, remove m, bind off 26 (26, 30, 32, 34, 36) sleeve sts, remove m, then knit across 26 (27, 30, 31, 33, 34) front sts.

Underarm Rnd: CO 6 (6, 6, 7, 7, 8) sts, place new BOR m, CO 5 (7, 6, 7, 7, 8) knit across 27

(27, 31, 31, 34, 34) back sts, bind off 26 (26, 30, 32, 34, 46) sleeve sts, remove m, using the backwards loop cast-on, CO 11 (13, 12, 14, 14, 16) sts, knit across 26 (27, 30, 31, 33, 34) front sts, knit to end of rnd.

Knit every rnd keeping the stripe pattern as established until piece measures 2 (2.5, 2.5, 3, 3.5, 4) in / 5 (6.5, 6.5, 7.5, 9, 10) cm from underarm.

Inc Rnd: *K4, k1f&b; rep form * to end of rnd— 90 (96, 102, 108, 114, 120) sts.

Continue to knit in the rnd until piece measures 6.5 (6.5, 7, 8, 8.5, 9) in / 16.5 (16.5, 18, 20.5, 21.5, 23) cm.

Back Shaping

Row 1 (RS): Bind off 8 (8, 8, 9, 10, 10) sts, k37 (40, 43, 45, 49, 52) sts. Place remaining 45 (48, 51, 54, 57, 60) sts on hold for front.

Row 2 (WS): Bind off 8 (8, 8, 9, 10, 10) sts, purl to end—29 (32, 35, 36, 37, 40) sts.

Work 6 (4, 0, 2, 2, 0) rows in flat St st.

Dec Row (RS): K1, ssk, knit to last 3 sts, k2tog, k1—2 sts decreased.

Even Row (WS): Purl

Repeat last 2 rows 3 (4, 5, 5, 5, 6) times more—
21 (22, 23, 24, 25, 26) sts.
Work in flat St st for 5 (5, 5, 5, 7, 7) rows. Bind
off all sts.

Front Shaping

Row 1 (RS): Bind off 10 (10, 12, 12, 14, 14) sts,
knit to end.
Row 2 (WS): Bind off 10 (10, 12, 12, 14, 14) sts,
purl to end—25 (28, 27, 30, 29, 32) sts.
Work 4 (0, 6, 2, 8, 4) rows in flat St st.
Dec Row (RS): K1, ssk, knit to last 3 sts, k2tog,
k1—2 sts decreased.
Even Row (WS): Purl.
Repeat last 2 rows 2 (3, 2, 3, 2, 3) times
more—19 (20, 21, 22, 23, 24) sts. Bind off all
sts knitwise.

Arm Edging

With CC, pick up 2 sts for every 3 sts
around armhole.
Inc Rnd: *K1, k1f&b; rep from * to end of row.
Work in St st for 3 rows.
Bind off all sts knitwise.

Neck Edging

With CC, pick up sts along neck edging (1 st for
every neck st). Bind off all sts knitwise.

Legs

With MC, pick up 2 sts for every 3 sts around
leg opening. **Inc Rnd:** *P1f&b; rep from *
across the row.
Next Rnd: Knit.
Next Rnd: Purl. Bind off all sts knitwise.

Skirt

With CC, about 2 in / 5 cm from underam, pick
up 1 st for every st around the entire piece.
Next Rnd: Knit.
Inc Rnd: *K1, k1f&b; rep from * to end of rnd.
Work in St st (knit every round) for 5
in / 12.5 cm
Bind off all sts knitwise.

FINISHING

Weave in all ends. Wash and block as desired.
Sew snap tape on opposite sides of
bottom flaps.

ABBREVIATIONS

BOR	beginning of round
CC	contrasting color
CO	cast on
dpn(s)	double-pointed needle(s)
k	knit
k1f&b	knit into the front and back of 1 st
k2tog	knit 2 sts together as 1 st
m	marker
m1L	Make 1 left: lift bar between sts from front to back with the left needle and then knit through the back of it with the right needle
m1R	Make 1 right: lift bar between sts from back to front with the left needle and then knit through the front of it with the right needle
MC	main color
p	purl
p1f&b	purl into the front and back of 1 st
pm	place marker
rep	repeat
rnd(s)	round(s)
sm	slip marker
ssk	slip, slip, knit
St st	Stockinette stitch
st(s)	stitch(es)
tog	together

YARN SOURCES

Destination Yarn
www.destinationyarn.com

The Fiber Seed
www.thefiberseed.com

Fibre Art Studio
www.etsy.com FibreArtStudio

Jilly & Kiddles
www.jillyandkiddles.com

Kim Dyes Yarn
www.kimdyesyarn.com

Knit One Crochet Too
www.knitonecrochettoo.com

Knit Picks
www.knitpicks.com

Lion Brand Yarn
www.lionbrand.com

Lorna's Laces
www.lornaslaces.net

Malabrigo Yarn
www.malabrigoyarn.com

Space Cadet Yarn Company
www.spacecadetyarn.com

SweetGeorgia Yarns
www.sweetgeorgiayarns.com

Tippy Tree Yarns
www.tippytreeyarns.com

DOLL
Waldorf Doll purchased from Bamboletta
www.bamboletta.com

ACKNOWLEDGMENTS

Goodness! This book has definitely been a lifelong dream and one roller coaster of a journey! It was inspired by my own youngest sweet little one, who is now a charming, inquisitive, and boundless ball-of-energy seven-year-old. I made the sketches and plans for this book while he would lie napping on me, just a mere two-month-old sweet bundle of joy. Writing this book and knitting the samples would never have been possible without the support of my family. They like to joke that I quarantined before it was cool (at least, when they aren't joking that I wrote and knit a book *before* quarantine).

My amazing technical editor, Corrina Ferguson, thank you! For holding my hand, and dealing with my last-minute rants and frantic texts. You are not only a fantastic editor but an even more incredible and invaluable friend.

My photographer, Kellie Nuss, I knew that if I ever did a book, there was no one I'd trust more with capturing the look than you! You are not only a talented photographer, but I am blessed to call you friend. Thank you for everything!

To the amazing Peloton community and instructors (especially Ally Love, Christine D'Ercole, Jess Sims, Kristin McGee, and Aditi), I am so incredibly grateful for the hands on my back always! It's an honor to be a part of this incredible community. You all have taught me that I can do hard things and that I have the courage to show up authentically, always.

Mike, you are my rock, my everything. Thanks for picking up the slack, for taking over when I just needed to tackle this project, and for always supporting me no matter how crazy or wild my plans are (I'm still waiting on that baby goat, though!!). Lilly Grace, Micah, Peter, Addison, and Sheldon, my own dear, sweet little monkeys, I love you to the moon and back. May you be inspired just a tiny bit to never, ever give up on your dreams, no matter how long it takes, and remember that how you do anything is how you do everything!

Most importantly, to God, my creator, my Designer, my Higher Power, for without whom none of this would be possible. I'm forever grateful to be a child of the King and to be enough just as I am.

VISUAL INDEX

The Basics

Basic Romper 2

Basic Stripes 6

Basic Hooded Romper 11

A Special Little Pocket 16

Basic Little Glowbug 21

Rainbow Stripes Onesie 25

Bamboletta Romper 29

Fun on the Farm

Sheep 34

Pig 39

Frog 44

Puppy 49

Fox 54

Cat 58

Cat Bamboletta Romper 62

Let's Visit the Zoo!

Giraffe 66

Lion 72

Elephant 77

Panda 84

Penguin 88

Flamingo 92

Mommy's Little Monkey 96

Let's Imagine!

Pumpkin 102

Dinosaur 107

Friendly Neighborhood Tiger or
Honey Bear 112

Unicorn 117

Alien 122

Ballerina 127